Incarnation

Incarnation

Reflections on Luke 1

P. D. GRAY

RESOURCE *Publications* • Eugene, Oregon

INCARNATION
Reflections on Luke 1

Copyright © 2025 P. D. Gray. All rights reserved. Except for brief quotations in critical publications or reviews, no part of this book may be reproduced in any manner without prior written permission from the publisher. Write: Permissions, Wipf and Stock Publishers, 199 W. 8th Ave., Suite 3, Eugene, OR 97401.

Resource Publications
An Imprint of Wipf and Stock Publishers
199 W. 8th Ave., Suite 3
Eugene, OR 97401

www.wipfandstock.com

PAPERBACK ISBN: 978-1-6667-8805-1
HARDCOVER ISBN: 978-1-6667-8806-8
EBOOK ISBN: 978-1-6667-8807-5

04/01/25

I would like to dedicate this book to those Christians in that ancient land of Syria, who are now living through times of new uncertainty and instability. May the Lord for Whom nothing is new, uncertain, or unstable, be their strength, even as we in the West cannot begin to fully empathize with them but, nevertheless, pity and pray for them.

"Therefore the Lord himself shall give you a sign; Behold, a virgin shall conceive, and bear a son, and shall call his name Immanuel" (Isa 7:14).

"But thou, Bethlehem Ephratah, *though* thou be little among the thousands of Judah, *yet* out of thee shall he come forth unto me *that is* to be ruler in Israel; whose goings forth *have been* from of old, from everlasting" (Mic 5:2).

Contents

	Author's note	ix

A GODLY KING (ISAIAH 39)

1	Dealing with the world wrongly—Isaiah 39:1–4	3
2	Judgment graciously accepted—Isaiah 39:5–8	6

GOD THE KING (ISAIAH 40:1–11)

3	The voice of the greatest man—Isaiah 40:1–5	11
4	Behold your God!—Isaiah 40:6–11	14

THE GREATEST MAN (LUKE 1:5–25)

5	A certain priest—Luke 1:5–7, 8–10	19
6	News of the best man—Luke 1:11–12, 13–15, 16–17	27
7	Blessings and rebukes—Luke 1:18–20, 21–22, 23–25	37

THE GOD-MAN (LUKE 1:26–56)

8	A highly favored virgin—Luke 1:26–28	51
9	The news foretold—Luke 1:29–33	56
10	A blessed dialogue—Luke 1:34–38	65
11	A great encounter—Luke 1:39–41, 42–45	76
12	A psalm out of time—Luke 1:46–47, 48–49, 50–56	87

Author's note

JUST AS IT IS unwise to over-emphasize any particular doctrine, verse of Scripture, or Person of the Godhead, so it is unhelpful to overly fixate on just one of Christ's fourfold victorious stages of salvation which, together combined, brought and bring such enormous blessing to the human race.

The 'empty tomb' is often fixated on on Resurrection Sunday / Easter Sunday, call it what you will. However, the *Resurrection* was preceded by the *Incarnation* and the *Crucifixion*; consequently proceeded by the *Ascension*. One might remember these by the acronym *ICRA*, so as to keep all four stages in view.

Moreover, one might also keep in mind that each stage was an extraordinary embodiment of humility and victory. The lowly stable-crib dwelling was a living rebuke to all that we would naturally lift up and esteem with geopolitical pomp and circumstance. Herod and Pilate would be those whom the natural man would see as important; movers and shakers who had made names for themselves. Christ's *Incarnation* victoriously rebuked our false assumptions. Who esteems Herod or Pilate today?

The *Crucifixion* has been seen by many as a tragic example of a good life cruelly hacked down by a vengeful, cynical world. However, it is more helpful to view it as the deliberate laying down of the Incarnate life in order to pay for the sins of millions who constitute the elect. It marked the final payment for the unjust (us) by the just (Christ) in order that our hope might no longer rest upon a future promise but upon an historical reality with eternal value.

AUTHOR'S NOTE

The *Resurrection* is sometimes viewed with sentimental pathos but was far more; the victorious rising up of our Conqueror of sin, death and hell. It was the Divine demolition of the kingdom of darkness which would thence have to contend with a global rather than local geographically based kingdom; now, the devil would increasingly have enemies from all races, tribes and tongues. As Christ arose, the global elect would arise throughout time with Him, often in the most unexpected of places.

The *Ascension* tends to be the most ignored of the fourfold victory of Christ during His earthly time of dwelling bodily among us. However, if Christ did not ascend, global Christian soldiers would not now be marching victoriously onward, in Him. From the Book of Acts onwards, the church, that is us if we are in Him, has been made able and willing to move forwards as our hope is locked fast in Him, our glorious Victor.

Let us now therefore examine the first of these four stages in greater depth.

A godly king

1

Dealing with the world wrongly

> "At that time Merodachbaladan, the son of Baladan, king of Babylon, sent letters and a present to Hezekiah: for he had heard that he had been sick, and was recovered. And Hezekiah was glad of them, and shewed them the house of his precious things, the silver, and the gold, and the spices, and the precious ointment, and all the house of his armour, and all that was found in his treasures: there was nothing in his house, nor in all his dominion, that Hezekiah shewed them not.
> Then came Isaiah the prophet unto king Hezekiah, and said unto him, What said these men? and from whence came they unto thee? And Hezekiah said, They are come from a far country unto me, even from Babylon. Then said he, What have they seen in thine house? And Hezekiah answered, All that is in mine house have they seen: there is nothing among my treasures that I have not shewed them." (Isa 39:1–4)

THERE IS A WAY which seems right in our eyes, in which we seem to be doing the best we can. It could be a promotion at work, a business deal, or some other thing of worldly advantage. However, for a believer all things need to be brought to the supernatural scanner of Scripture so that we may "prove all things; hold fast that which is good." (1 Thess 5:21). Many things which seem good are not.

Such was Hezekiah's predicament in his day of personal and national sickness. The Lord had graciously healed him of his terrible, life-threatening illness; however, rather than dealing with the world from a position of strength as King Solomon did re the Queen of Sheba, Hezekiah in his heart dealt with the Babylonian envoys in a man-pleasing, pathetically weak way. Despite many redeeming qualities and past triumphs, this godly ruler sadly dishonoured the Lord and was revealed to have been operating in accord with the flesh rather than the Spirit.

We are commanded to "seek ye first the kingdom of God, and his righteousness; and all these things shall be added unto you" (Matt 6:33). Hezekiah instead became entangled with worldly assurances, promises and approval, forgetting the Lord who had miraculously healed him. He forgot the principle of two kingdoms; that the kingdom of this world is at war with the kingdom of God, and that Hezekiah was supposed to be the man of God, defending the interests of the Eternal who had redeemed his nation from the depths of slavery in worldly Egypt. God in His Fatherly wisdom, "left him, to try him, that he might know all *that was* in his heart" (2 Chr 32:31).

Are we any better? If left to our own devices, would we too not seek the comfort, approval and acceptance of this world? If, for example, I were to be offered a lucrative book deal with a slick, global 'Christian' publishing giant and be tempted by the chance to influence the world, would I not in fleshly wisdom seek to make peace with the world and shave off those jarring sparks of fiery Gospel truth? Would I be one who would honour and preserve the things of God, separating them from the things of the world, or would I rather give "that which is holy unto the dogs" (Matt 7:6)? In Hezekiah's case, he was foolishly friendly and unwisely dependent upon spiritual 'dogs' and 'swine' who would in due course 'trample' the people of God and take them into captivity.

Isaiah, in the Spirit, dealt with Hezekiah firmly, allowing Hezekiah to articulate exactly what he had done. If his initial sin of pride was dealt with personally, this new sin of dealing with the kingdom of the world wrongly had public ramifications. The nation would be judged, for the king represented the people. Gone was the old zeal and fervour of Solomon's day in which evangelistic fire ushered in people from far countries and sent them away full of wonder and awe. It was now a time in which the outward kingdom of God was ready to do ungodly deals with the world—to compromise, to look to worldly ways to bring about blessed results. Neither hot nor cold, their lukewarmness was an affront to God.

We too must flee from a lukewarm religion of outward deals and cowardly, man-centred approval. The religion of which God approves is rarely accepted or liked by the world, for it is fearless, zealous, forthright, irritating to our downward proclivity for fleshly comfort. We are to be spiritual foot soldiers, heavenly-minded ambassadors, a kingdom of praying priests, a royal, biblical priesthood.

Honour the true King, whoever you are, and you will not go astray. Honour the false king of worldliness and you will end up being despised by both kingdoms—man's and God's; "good for nothing, but to be cast out and to be trodden under foot of men" (Matt 5:13).

2

Judgment graciously accepted

> "Then said Isaiah to Hezekiah, Hear the word of the LORD of hosts: Behold, the days come, that all that *is* in thine house, and *that* which thy fathers have laid up in store until this day, shall be carried to Babylon: nothing shall be left, saith the LORD. And of thy sons that shall issue from thee, which thou shalt beget, shall they take away; and they shall be eunuchs in the palace of the king of Babylon.
> Then said Hezekiah to Isaiah, Good *is* the word of the LORD which thou hast spoken. He said moreover, For there shall be peace and truth in my days." (Isa 39:5–8)

HEZEKIAH WAS A BELIEVER; overall, a good king whose name has to do with strength. This should not be lost sight of, even as the Scriptures put this last part of his life under divine scrutiny. We must see the bigger picture; the fact that this saved king was being juxtaposed against the King of kings, the Lord Jesus Christ who is so vividly exalted in the latter half of the Book of Isaiah.

As the sun rises, so the moon must fade into the background. John the Baptist, alluded to in the very next chapter, knew he must decrease; so must all our religion which does not magnify, exalt and focus on the supremacy and excellence of the Lord Jesus Christ.

In the "house" of Reformed Christianity, which many in our day rightly revere and appreciate, we have "laid up in store" many golden works of theology; many tomes of mighty doctrines helpfully explained. We have many masters of Hebrew, Greek and Latin; we are grateful and amazed that the Lord has raised up spiritual giants over centuries. And yet, the sobering question remains, "lovest thou me more than these?" (John 21:15), and "lovest thou me?" (v. 16), then . . . "lovest thou me?" (v. 17)!

The probing evaluations of the seven churches in Revelation 2 and 3 also talk of having "left thy first love" (Rev 2:4) and forgetting that by nature we are "wretched, and miserable, and poor, and blind, and naked" (Rev 3:17). Yet, if we are the Lord's, He will bring us back to view what we are, that we may turn once more to base our hope on the promised Seed of the woman, remembering that in Him there is a 'not guilty' verdict for all who believe.

"Babylon" was both a literal empire and symbolic representation of the world perpetually opposed to God. All who turn to this power and put their trust in it will ultimately become fruitless and bereft; "nothing shall be left" of eternal value. Instead of becoming adopted children of God, Babylon will leave us "eunuchs," devoid of the vivifying, fructifying truth of Christ. Even our very best works and prized heritage will count for nothing in the end, if we are not looking to the true Author and Finisher of our faith.

We may be looking to Calvin or to Spurgeon and be going to hell, not because anything was wrong with them but because we locate glory and honour in man rather than God. The "king of Babylon" or, perhaps for us, outward religion, can lead us astray, seducing us into believing we are doing all for God's glory. Much searching of heart is required lest we end up like the builder who could not complete his tower because he did not "counteth the cost" (Luke 14:28) of leaving worldliness in all its forms, false religion being one of the hardest to expose and eschew.

Hezekiah was a godly man and so submitted to divine Providence, revealed to him through the prophet Isaiah. What a blessing when we receive God's word from the preaching of the pulpit rather than being distracted from or hostile towards it. We ought not merely hear but seek to apply it to our own lives. "Good *is* the word of the Lord" precisely because God is good. He is wholly good and therefore cannot do anything which is not good. It might have been that Hezekiah was grateful for those remaining blessings and a divine delaying of the terrible judgments to come. It could also have been that he was hoping against hope that the judgment would be rescinded.

Being a godly man who was looking for the promise of the Seed, it is possible that Hezekiah contented himself that "peace" and "truth" were to be preached and magnified in his "days"; perhaps the prophet's wonderful, soaring revelations of Immanuel's two comings, first and second, would be granted sooner rather than later, even though some outwardly challenging and tough times would lie ahead for the nation of Israel.

Likewise, no one living in the West would like to see the West crumble and fall; still, we know that this is what we deserve. We fear those terrible portraits of last day judgments seen in successive snapshots in the Book of Revelation. Nevertheless, we know that such things must come to pass and so we look by faith to eternity when that "king of Babylon" will finally be fully crushed, never to raise his baleful head again and all our tears shall be wiped away for good.

God the King

3

The voice of the greatest man

"Comfort ye, comfort ye my people, saith your God. Speak ye comfortably to Jerusalem, and cry unto her, that her warfare is accomplished, that her iniquity is pardoned: for she hath received of the LORD'S hand double for all her sins.
 The voice of him that crieth in the wilderness, Prepare ye the way of the LORD, make straight in the desert a highway for our God. Every valley shall be exalted, and every mountain and hill shall be made low: and the crooked shall be made straight, and the rough places plain: and the glory of the LORD shall be revealed, and all flesh shall see it together: for the mouth of the LORD hath spoken *it*." (Isa 40:1–5)

WE CANNOT SAY THAT the world is 'good', at least not in the way it was at the dawn of Creation. Since the Fall of Man (Genesis 3), manifold sparks of strife have deeply troubled the human race; a bitter fact which fills all newspapers everywhere, every day. Not only is "comfort," therefore, such a necessary and desperately needed thing but true comfort, we learn, is only found in "our God."

For all Hezekiah's human "goodness" (2 Chr 32:32) and "honor" (v. 33), the "people" of God must look to God, regardless of human instruments. We must not seek to get soul "comfort" from our pastor, although the Holy Spirit speaking through the preaching of our pastor graciously uses him to give us comfort as he adheres to the true and living word.

We, like 8th century BC "Jerusalem," must not be content with any outward form of religion which doesn't deal with the soul's need; the need for its "warfare" to be "accomplished" and its "iniquity" to be "pardoned." We must ask, seek and knock until it is well with our souls. We can only get this by looking unto Jesus. And even when this assurance is ours, still the warfare surrounds us; still the iniquity dismays us; yet, with a new, spiritual nature, we have the strength to endure the battle which once compressed and destroyed.

Here too is the prophetic reference to none other than the best man of the entire Old Testament—John the Baptist. He would be the immediate forerunner and professor of Jesus, the final and greatest prophet, graciously granted such blessed proximity to Jesus, even from the womb. We might often wonder at the scant information provided about this final and best prophet; yet, this in itself bespeaks the extent to which he was utterly and willingly consumed by the love of the Lord Jesus; closer to him than any other, BC.

We are treated also to an insight into John the Baptist's preaching. We might wonder at what drew souls into the "wilderness" to hear this greatest man speak. It would seem that it was the simplicity and Christ-exalting nature of his words; "Prepare"; "make straight." Just as Hezekiah was commanded to get his house in order, so the crowds who flocked to hear John preach. It was stark, godly, powerful preaching, without compromise or an unedifying focus on worldly comfort.

Our hearts are to repent of their waywardness; our minds to look to something greater than anything the kingdoms of this world can deliver. All riches, honors and accolades melt into nothingness and triviality; "every mountain" of worldliness is a pathetic wrinkle in God's sight; every "crooked" obstacle which worries, frustrates and baffles worldly man is to "be made straight" by the Lord. Soli Deo Gloria was John the Baptist's message, and the Holy

Spirit applied it to multitudes; to "all flesh" from all kinds of backgrounds, statuses, and age-groups. The word of God should never be seen as only for one sort of people; it applies to all, even though it will not be received by all.

4

Behold your God!

"The voice said, Cry. And he said, What shall I cry? All flesh *is* grass, and all the goodliness thereof *is* as the flower of the field: The grass withereth, the flower fadeth: because the spirit of the LORD bloweth upon it: surely the people *is* grass. The grass withereth, the flower fadeth: but the word of our God shall stand for ever.

O Zion, that bringest good tidings, get thee up into the high mountain; O Jerusalem, that bringest good tidings, lift up thy voice with strength; lift *it* up, be not afraid; say unto the cities of Judah, Behold your God! Behold, the Lord GOD will come with strong *hand*, and his arm shall rule for him: behold, his reward *is* with him, and his work before him. He shall feed his flock like a shepherd: he shall gather the lambs with his arm, and carry *them* in his bosom, *and* shall gently lead those that are with young." (Isa 40:6–11)

THE VOICE OF GOD speaks through the voice of man. Every Lord's day it is the Lord's voice which resounds when God's word is faithfully opened and proclaimed. The preacher of God's word often takes on a new power and becomes larger than life in the pulpit; then, after the sermon, becomes himself again.

Here, we see ahead of time the faithful man of God preaching in full flow; "All flesh *is* grass," and are awed by the majesty, simplicity and depth of such a statement. It is true on so many levels; on the physical, it speaks of mortality; on the political, of man's foolish pride; on the spiritual, it speaks of man's inability to stand upright before God except by faith in a Substitute.

We have just seen a great and godly king, Hezekiah, who like all men, even godly ones, was disappointing to some degree. Such "goodliness" as he had, as all believers have, is nothing less than the Holy Spirit taking up residence within, inclining thoughts and ways which are not of the flesh. We have treasure in this sense, but in our own right remain as "grass"; flimsy, temporary, replaceable. Our lifespans were reduced to three-score and ten; our Tower of Babel and universal language was frustrated and fragmented by the sovereign will of God who "bloweth upon" all our plans which are not "rooted and built up in him" (Col 2:7).

Every thought, word, and breath of man ought to be giving glory to our Creator. We resent this and even those who do have faith can become lazy, proud and complacent about the miraculous and sustaining work of the Holy Spirit within . . . "but the word of our God shall stand for ever," the wilderness preacher continues, and thanks be to God that this is so. Thanks be to God that our Bibles are rock-solid, that the Word Incarnate, Jesus Christ, descended, lived, died and rose for such unworthy "grass" as us. Because Christ "shall stand for ever," unworthy Christians by grace "shall stand for ever." Where He is, so are we.

The Baptist's sermons were full of Christ, as indicated in this portion of them recorded here. God's people operate from a position of strength, not weakness, their strength being the LORD. When thinking upon and living upon Him, we stand upon "the high mountain," looking down at the doomed kingdoms of this world and praying for souls to be delivered therefrom. When thinking on and praying in the Spirit, we have real "strength," believing our imperfect prayers to be being received in the courts of heaven, mediated and perfected by our High Priest. When looking unto Jesus, we have no fear. When looking elsewhere, we start to sink.

"Behold your God!" We are to treat each day as a Christmas day in which we remember the Incarnation. We marvel at His condescension; at the fact that despite having all power over creation, He deigned to descend to our level, to rub shoulders with us, to pray for, encourage, guide and uplift us. In and of ourselves we are flimsy; in Christ we are as precious sheep whom "He shall feed," whom "He shall gather" from all corners of history and geography.

In Him we are never alone, for He carries us "in his bosom." He has the highest regard for women; He would, after all, be miraculously conceived in a chosen woman. And He blesses burdened pastors, deacons, mothers and fathers who "are with young" people. He blesses congregations who support those who are young and inexperienced in the faith.

He is altogether to be worshipped and glorified—to be read about, thought upon, meditated on and prayed to. He is the greatest and ultimate subject of every sermon worth hearing—the chief means and end of every godly hymn and prayer. Blessed be His name, as we now seek to trace His story, from Heaven to earth, in the Incarnation.

But let us first dwell a bit longer upon His ordained forerunner, John.

The greatest man

5

A certain priest

> "There was in the days of Herod, the king of Judaea, a certain priest named Zacharias, of the course of Abia: and his wife *was* of the daughters of Aaron, and her name *was* Elisabeth. And they were both righteous before God, walking in all the commandments and ordinances of the Lord blameless. And they had no child, because that Elisabeth was barren, and they both were *now* well stricken in years" (Luke 1:5–7)

HEROD AND ZACHARIAS MAY dwell together in this verse but are now surely separated forever. What a tangled web of deceit, megalomania and wickedness the former wove; what a godly legacy of patience, reverence and acceptance the latter left. Here on earth, we are very much in Herod's realm; short-lived and doomed to destruction.

Originating from Idumea (or Edom), this Herod (Herod the Great, so-called) didn't have the right to occupy an office of Jewish power in that blessed region of Judaea. He was also bankrolled by the Romans and had a complicated and murderous personal life in which he trusted and was trusted by no one. What an awful man to be placed in close proximity to godly old Zacharias; how contrary are God's ways to ours and how fickle we are when we give too much of our attention to the egomaniacal so-called great ones of our age, barely giving our pastor more than an hour of time on a Sunday.

Unlike in the media, political and academic spheres, where so-called great ones are put in the spotlight, here it is Zacharias who is given prominence and remembered, his name meaning God (*Yah*) remembers (*zakar*). Herod may have had access to all that this world has to offer, but Zacharias had God in his life, tracing his lineage back to that original division of Aaron's sons hundreds of years before him. Equally, his wife could trace herself back to the priestly line of Aaron.

Bloodlines do not save, though, and so each personally, by grace, was given genuine faith, the fruits thereof being humility of mind, contentment of soul, lively attendance to the manifold duties of temple worship, accepting the will of God in that they were not granted a child of their own.

Meanwhile, the Machiavellian manoeuvrings of Herod's political pawns were intensifying, leaving many either dead or scarred. So it is in our day, in which the corridors of power never lead to inward peace. That is not to say that Zacharias and his wife were having everything their hearts desired. Nevertheless, they had God and were therefore complete. What a thing it is to be complete!

Elisabeth's name (*el* – God, *shaba*—to swear or 'seven') has an internal promise within it in which God's oath would be the thing she could trust, not the glitz or glamour of the world, nor the prestige and power of external religion. Of course she had always wanted a child of her own, but by faith submitted her will to the Lord's.

Zacharias, too, would humble himself in the system of priestly administration, the temple worship wisely using a system of lots, nipping in the bud any inklings of resentment or jealousy. Moreover, the privilege of a lifetime, offering incense, would be granted just once so that a maximal number would get their turn and none could boast in human attainment or advancement.

IMPUTED AND IMPARTED

The yearly Passover would have reminded them of the fact that were it not for God's passing over their sins and looking upon them through the paradigm of a heavenly Substitute and blood offering, they would have no right to claim relationship with God. Their righteousness was therefore first and foremost a righteousness "before" or "in the presence of" God. He it was who gave it them; He would be the ground of their confidence.

Because of righteousness imputed, they had righteousness imparted, which would animate their hours, day by day. The believer, having no confidence in the flesh, instead rejoices by faith that they may be found "walking in" the moral law of God, the law which has been kept on their behalf by the Holy One of Israel, which they incrementally learn to appreciate and fulfil, never consistently or fully.

How close they were, temporally, to the incarnation of Christ and yet they were no closer than we are, for our faith does not depend on geographical or historical nearness to Christ in the flesh but rather on the spiritual enlivening of the Holy Spirit within, He who transcends time and space. A spiritual, God-given faith must precede a walk of holiness. Thankfully, where the former is, in time the latter will come.

They were not those who skimped on the outward or robbed God of the necessary communal regulations of temple worship, such as it was. Their hearts delighted inwardly because of the presence of God; their bodies outwardly in fulfilling the various duties required of those Levitical Jews whose duty it was to administer daily sacrifices on the altar, keep the incense burning, clean, repair and maintain all the many requirements of the house of God, such as it was (the temple or tabernacle is now a vastly enlarged spiritual structure which spans the globe).

GOD REMEMBERS AND GOD SWEARS

A thing of sadness it is to have no "child," seeing that children give so much joy and are believed to be a divine blessing; in their day even more than in our own, barrenness would be seen as evidence of God's disfavor. However, no hint of blame is attached to this godly old couple; nor is there any bitterness revealed for our instruction. Such was their faith that as their names implied—God remembers & God swears—they were not tied to the outward but the inward . . . in love with God in their souls, on fire for Him, joyfully yielding their lives to His will and His people.

"Barren" ought to be seen without eyes of judgment. We cannot help but remember the births of Samson, Samuel, and Isaac, all of whom were given to people of faith, against human expectation. Even if such apparently "barren" souls had not been granted children, they would have been content to live upon the promises of God, looking to the coming of the Messianic Seed, anticipating an acceptance among an innumerable family of blood-bought heavenly-minded saints. To be physically barren is one thing; spiritually barren another. If you have faith then all things are yours. If you have it not, you are damned.

"Stricken" for us carries rather more negative connotations than intended in the original, just as with "barren." To be old in the world's way of thinking is to be cursed with less vigor, energy and strength to enjoy the pleasures of the body. Such is not the case for believers who graciously grow in wisdom and grace over the years. Apart from a few notable exceptions, the majority of godly heroes of the faith have been in middle or older age; pointing us to heaven in which we will be living forever, learning about and enjoying the presence of God ceaselessly, without boredom or frustration in resurrected bodies with never-tiring minds. If the earth fears the ageing process, the heavenly-earth will exist with an endless but incorruptible ageing of ever-living saints. It is hard to comprehend but by faith we accept.

THE PRIEST'S OFFICE

> "And it came to pass, that while he executed the priest's office before God in the order of his course, according to the custom of the priest's office, his lot was to burn incense when he went into the temple of the Lord. And the whole multitude of the people were praying without at the time of incense" (Luke 1:8–10).

We know what an imprecise tool language can be, for although "it came to pass" we know that nothing just comes to pass, strictly speaking, for God foreknows, ordains, orchestrates all the providences of our lives. God created Zacharias and placed him right there at that exact moment in time, with the means of fulfilling the religious duties of his day.

Apparently, there were four lots, the third one involving the handling of holy incense which would typify the ultimate incense of Christ's prayers on His people's behalf. Due to the large numbers of priests and the solemnity of the ritual, this was Zacharias' one and only time of being granted this privilege, and he would have done it to the utmost of his ability, not wanting to get anything wrong.

It is no less important in our day to be people who physically congregate, who do not forsake the assembling of ourselves without just cause. Revivals and blessings of previous centuries have not just come "to pass," but have come largely through faithful men and women of God who gave themselves to lively prayer and godly congregation.

We professing Christians each occupy "the priest's office" precisely because our High Priest has ascended into glory. Zacharias wouldn't have entered into the holy of holies; only the holy place. Likewise, we of faith have a right to be baptized and partake in the Lord's table. We also have a right to pray to our Father in heaven, believing our prayers to be accepted in the perpetual incense of Christ the Beloved's prayers for us. We have a more direct access to God in which the elaborate rituals of Zacharias' day are, through Christ, fulfilled.

Zacharias was someone who did things by the Book, without innovation or worldly compromise. He was operating on God's terms for he genuinely believed that everything he did, especially when it came to corporate worship, was "before God." When we physically attend our local church, does it feel like we are entering into the very presence of God? It should, for if our worship is not before God then it is before men, and becomes merely a performance.

We live in an age of megachurch showmen and religious charlatans; yet Zacharias, as with so many others down the ages, was raised for the role he fulfilled and faithfully walked "in the order of his course," joyfully and gratefully, not perfunctorily or begrudgingly. Whether Baptist, Presbyterian, Methodist or other, God delights in those who are whole-hearted in their religion, who do not merely go through the motions or give only a part of themselves in worship but who are all in, seeking before all else to honor their Heavenly Father.

ONE'S LOT IN LIFE

We in the West live in an age that despises tradition; an age in which individuals are invited to sneer at historical heritage and become proud rebels without a cause; rejecting those time-honored principles which have led us into ways of order, harmony, godly restraint. Such was not the case with godly Zacharias. He looked forward to the official channels of worship; he revered the customs by which he was raised in which he was privileged to hold the priest's office, something stretching to the times of patriarchs.

Our age tells us you can worship God on your own terms and can blithely ignore any wisdom given to giants of the faith who went before us; we can wear our jeans and our t-shirts whilst jumping up and down to soft-rock music, claiming to speak in tongues; whatever feels right is right. We are told that those who wear conservative clothing and worship in reverent orderliness are legalists, formalists, cold-hearted pharisees. It is certain, however, that Zacharias would have had more in common with the latter than the former.

Zacharias' "lot" in life was to burn incense, to participate in that holy team of priests who would keep the incense going, day and night, in submission to the Holy One in heaven. It is our lot, too, for we as the global, Jewish-Gentile church of Christ are to regularly keep offering up our prayers of praise, thanksgiving, confessions and supplications. If you have any spare time, as well as necessary rest and relaxation, the best thing you could do would be to offer up the incense of prayer; you will never be the worse for it.

"His lot," then, was sufficient for him and he accepted it; godly contentedness is great gain. It might be your lot in life to go through some strange and discomfiting experiences; to 'suffer the slings and arrows of outrageous fortune', as the poet has said. But because you are a believer you have access to the throne of God through Christ our High Priest. You may have the certainty that you are exactly where God would have you—that all things are leading you to the place of eternal glory.

As Zacharias embraced his holy entering into the temple, what must his emotions have been. We must not underestimate, judge or slight the quiet, conservative Bible believers who go about things in a patient, methodical manner. They are, after all, entering the presence of God the moment they close their eyes and pray. Christ, too, would be slow to enter into the temple of a human body with which He would enter into the true Holy of holies—heaven, on our behalf; there to minister for His people on earth.

TO BURN INCENSE

We look with awe at this holy time; firstly, noticing how it was indeed "the whole multitude of the people," not part of them, for when God looks down upon His people, He sees the whole—the *body* of which Christ Jesus is the *head*. The whole multitude of believers upon earth is united in Him. The "people," moreover, reminds us of that important gift of humility, for we are ever ready to look to the left or right, comparing ourselves with others, when we should be looking up. Rather than vying with each other, if we were to judge ourselves more on the vertical (Godward) than horizontal (manward) we would be more willing to serve God sincerely; each other with more charitable consideration.

"Praying" is the one thing that characterizes God's people for, like a baby, a Christian who never prays is like a baby who never breathes, never cries. The prayers of God's people in the universal church are perpetual; prefigured here. What happened typically and locally through the priest Zacharias now occurs globally and continuously through Christ the Priest of priests. It behooves us to remember how the tabernacle and temple of old didn't just prefigure the New Testament order of things; rather, the New Testament order of things is patterned on the true nature of the spiritual temple in heaven, while those Old Testament Mosaic and Davidic/Solomonic iterations were earthly and limited manifestations of what is in heaven. Testaments old and new both point to our heavenly home in which perfect, true worship begins and ends.

As long as we are reading these words on paper or screen, we are "without," outside heaven's gates. Our priest, the Priest, ministers in those eternal courts of glory, mediating between us and our Father. We may offer up prayers to God at any time of day and night; however, without Priest Jesus our efforts are in vain. He it is who goes about the duties of the heavenly temple continually, our prayers rising up towards and through Him. The "time of incense" which Zacharias was privileged to minister but once in his lifetime exists in Christ perpetually, until the end of this fallen order.

And what of this mysterious and holy incense itself. Well, we learn in Exodus that it was to be composed of a peculiar mixture of five ingredients which was never to be used outside of the holy temple, five often being associated with that most blessed doctrine—*grace*.

6

News of the best man

> "And there appeared unto him an angel of the Lord standing on the right side of the altar of incense. And when Zacharias saw *him*, he was troubled, and fear fell upon him." (Luke 1:11–12).

WE ARE UTTERLY DEPENDENT on revelation, be it God the Son dealing directly with a man like Moses or through the intermediary messenger-role of an angel of the Lord, as in this case. Angels themselves are as dependent on God as we are; in 1 Peter 1:12 we read of the interest that angels have to "look into" God's dealings with His image-bearers who dwell in this sin-sick world, but they have their station and cannot enter the human experience.

As Zacharias was standing, "an angel" was "standing" because both were servants of God. The angel "appeared" in the human world, as the human will dwell in the angelic world—united in service to Christ. Interestingly, the angel (Gabriel), whose name means *mighty (man) of God*, was standing "on the right side," i.e., the side which had the shewbread, rather than the left side with the lampstand. Gabriel was on the side of bread-dependent man—a creature like us; vastly superior, but aligned. Christ the light or "lamp" of the world was yet to be born.

Angels are commonly referred to as messengers, heralds; at times, destroyers. They do not, however, have divinity within themselves but are charged with various responsibilities and tasks which occasionally manifest in an open way in the lives of humans. If the lampstand speaks of God shining in those made spiritually alive, the bread speaks of the bodily necessities of man in this world of weakness and exigency.

Perhaps it had been the case that the angel was there all along and, like Elisha who prayed that his servant's eyes be opened, even human priests were not spiritually minded enough to have any consciousness of angelic presence. More probable was it that this lofty angel descended from those heavenly courts to fulfill a specific mission re Zacharias.

Like Christ Himself, the greater would condescend to the lesser. There is a marked contrast, moreover, between angelic purity and obedience and Zacharias' fear, hesitancy and unbelief.

FEAR

Having to do with God is a fearful and life-changing experience; fearful in the best of senses. There have been accounts of ordained ministers of God's word who at some point in their ministry actually discovered the Lord for themselves. That day, as with all believers, was one of change, a radical re-making of identity; that which gives a person grounds for believing they have encountered the Divine and been converted.

It is, though, easy to lose the power of such an experience over time. Believing Zacharias, remembered of God, is here sharpened, awoken again to something of God's power and glory through a Divine messenger. Interestingly, it arouses in Zacharias a troubled and fearful response. Why?

A troubled conscience is the first reason, for there is no greater troubler of the mind than this; no greater protestor of misdeeds or witnesser of wrong thoughts. The world may go about its worldly business and the devil may win his battles; yet the sins of us grieve us the most. If we were as one of the unfallen angels, there would be nothing but joyful recognition when greeted by one of our own. However, it is because we are so far from being angelic that Zacharias' own sense of shortcomings come to the fore, for our instruction.

A second reason which can be gleaned from the subsequent verse is a fear which Zacharias may have had of presumptuously praying not just for a son but for the Seed to be born. At this time the Seed of Genesis had yet to be made incarnate and it was hoped with every new birth that this would be the One. We too might be praying for great things; revivals, for instance; but what if a revival were to come? We might feel unworthy and blameworthy for praying for such great things, imperfect and weak as we are, in and of ourselves. Who are we to pray for such a thing? Who are we to believe we could handle the reality of it.

A third reason, something even stronger than a troubled conscience—the sheer terror and fear of coming into the presence of the messenger of the holy, all-knowing, all-powerful God. This was no trifling encounter but a holy and *awe*ful event. It points us to the much greater fear of coming into the presence of Almighty God when that final Day arrives. How every mouth shall be stopped and every knee shall bow. How even the hardened, calloused Roman centurions were blown back as if by a powerful gust of wind when gentle Jesus merely declared His Divine 'I am' before them. But that was still within the Day of salvation. This final day will be altogether different, "for the great day of his wrath is come; and who shall be able to stand?" (Rev 6:17).

Who can fathom the holy *otherness* of the Creator when we creatures come into His presence. His is a terrifying and alarming greatness, a breath-taking power full of a glory, light, depth, omniscience and omnipotence that no creature can encounter without an element of fear.

SOME SHALLS

> "But the angel said unto him, Fear not, Zacharias: for thy prayer is heard; and thy wife Elisabeth shall bear thee a son, and thou shalt call his name John. And thou shalt have joy and gladness; and many shall rejoice at his birth. For he shall be great in the sight of the Lord, and shall drink neither wine nor strong drink; and he shall be filled with the Holy Ghost, even from his mother's womb" (Luke 1:13–15).

What wonderful words to hear from God's anointed messenger Zacharias who, despite all his misgivings about himself, is simply commanded to "Fear not." What a relief. We too can put ourselves in his shoes and rest assured that for all our worrying, soul searching and self-examining, our Father in heaven commands us to "Fear not." We are not to be unsure with regard to our salvation status. We are not in the hands of a capricious, vindictive, easily angered Roman or Greek 'god', but rather the true and living, loving Heavenly Father who is longsuffering towards us, who is full of pity and mercy, withholding nothing that is for our spiritual good.

Our God is a prayer-hearing and prayer-answering God; He is the One who will listen to us like no other can or will. He has taken account of our prayers before creation was conceived; while in a sense they are ordained, in another sense He delights to hear and respond to them, as if they were the fresh intentions of our own hearts rather than the beautiful manifestation of the Holy Spirit working within. No believer is alone, after all, but is prompted, inclined to read God's word, moved to repent and have faith, centered not on their doings but God's. The angel speaks to Zacharias by name, just as you are known by God as a unique, individual soul—as you.

The Lord delights in helping us through our lives' affairs, even down to the level of physical health, mental wellbeing and providential openings and closures. We are also to pray for great things such as the salvation of souls, even our enemies' souls, the turning around of nations, the return of our Lord Jesus Christ. We shouldn't hold back—prayers for the smaller along with the greater things. Amid the many storms and musings and doubts, the Lord gives us many a "shall" and "shalt" in which to rest.

A son would indeed be born to Zacharias and Elisabeth; not the Seed of Genesis 3; nevertheless, the greatest of Old Testament prophets, so close to Christ in many ways. John would be his name; 'Yah Is Gracious' or 'Yah Has Been Gracious'. A mighty privilege would be theirs, for this son would herald and point souls to the Son of Man, the Seed for which all of creation had been groaning since the Fall.

BIRTH

Any birth is a cause for joy; a micro-cosmos of the original *genesis* when something came *ex nihilo*. Yet there must be a spiritual birth as well as an earthly birth for each of us, else we have no hope of heaven which is a spiritual place. Joy is there at the earthly birth of a baby, although true and abiding joy exists only at their spiritual birth; only that will outlive the grave and make the sunset of our years filled with holy hope and heavenly anticipation.

"Gladness" in our day has a somewhat milder and less trenchant tone than joy, which somehow seems stronger, more heartfelt. However, in biblical usage it conveys a meaning of 'exultation, extreme joy, gladness', and so is an intensification of the more ordinary sense of joy experienced by every new parent upon earthly, physical birth.

How much more would *this* particular birth be for Zacharias and Elisabeth. This was no ordinary child but the very best of men—one who would be granted proximity to the Son of Man whose birth would overlap and utterly eclipse his. John was the best man but a man at best. Jesus was the perfect man, the second Adam, the Savior, God incarnate.

Despite his womb godliness, his relative merit, his comparative goodness, in himself John would be insufficient to make atonement for the never-dying soul of himself, let alone another. No prophet was greater, but the cause of his greatness lay outside of him, in his identification with another—the uncreated Son of God, born to die and conquer death. When people would try to identify John as the Seed, we are reminded that he was but a "man sent from God," "a witness . . . of the Light," but fundamentally like us, a saved-sinner, "not that Light" (John 1:8–10).

We rejoice in the lives of godly men and women in our day; spiritual guardians, elders, pastors, deacons, teachers, mothers, fathers, missionaries, evangelists and brethren. As with John, though, the cause of our rejoicing is that they have been eclipsed and overshadowed by the Savior who shepherds them, making them "great" to us.

"GREAT"

How mis-used is the term "great" in modern days; how we have both degraded it from what it once meant, and attributed to unworthy, material things the term "great," falling so short of what is "great" in God's sight. Where the Lord evaluates the heart, man evaluates the building, the discovery, the genius or world record. Many have been the so-called "great" ones of this world who, in God's sight, are not "great" but greatly sinful, greatly rebellious, forever cut off from the things of God.

Such was not the case with this John, however, for he was "great" in terms of being right with God. As Samuel was to be the first prophet and last judge of Israel, John was to be the last prophet and the chosen precursor to God incarnate; both Samuel and John abode by a Nazirite vow from birth. The wine, grooming and fashions of this world were not for them, for they were looking to a higher source of richness which would be a blessing to their souls forever.

Where this world covets lifestyle, consumption, wealth and health, these first and last men coveted the coming Messiah. The kingdom they were praying for was not of this world and their greatness was not, on the whole, recognized or accepted by a world which creates sandcastle after sandcastle of Babel-like ego-towers.

Greatness is a sobering thought, for if we are honest and search our souls, the desire to be great in the sight of man is probably more in us than we would care to admit. Even the fact that the vast majority of us was converted once outside the womb is of significance; it takes a lifetime to process and overcome our pre-converted lives by grace, whereas John had, mercifully, merely a few months in the womb before the Holy Ghost would take up residence within, blessing and sanctifying him for His distinct and holy purpose.

We should not make a Jesus out of John, nor elevate one saint over another. We professors of faith should seek to examine ourselves each day, evaluating our own smallness yet greatness in God's sight. In self, small; in Christ, great.

SOBERING AND CHASTENING

> "And many of the children of Israel shall he turn to the Lord their God. And he shall go before him in the spirit and power of Elias, to turn the hearts of the fathers to the children, and the disobedient to the wisdom of the just; to make ready a people prepared for the Lord" (Luke 1:16–17).

When we think of the mighty Abraham, Jacob, Joseph and David etc., the Bible declares John the Baptist to be the greatest of all. No one has surpassed him, the God-man excepted. Even so, his sobering and chastening message of repentance was largely ignored and despised. Who likes it! It is surely an unwelcome and unpalatable truth to the flesh; we would rather encourage ourselves by revisiting our rags to riches narratives of old. We do not like to dwell for long upon our present failings, our own need for daily soul searching, heart examination, sincere confession, contrition and cleansing. Nevertheless, to the believer it is necessary and health-giving. To the unbeliever, it is the call of death to the worldly life; it calls us to die and to be raised anew. It is a truly radical message.

What a shocking thing John's message must have been to the Jews of old. 'Who me!?' you can imagine many an upright, outwardly religious Jew saying. 'You're saying that *I*, a child of Abraham, need repentance? How dare you!' Such thoughts must have crossed the minds of many in John's day. It is no different today. Sermons which point the finger, apply the sword of Scripture to our own shortcomings, reveal our indwelling sin-natures, are generally not popular or well-received. They are especially despised by those who are outwardly religious, due to the goodness they feel they have built up over the years.

We read in Galatians 5 that the principle of sin within, the *flesh* so-called, is not just a hindrance to be once overcome in the Spirit, but is actively at war within us throughout our pilgrimage on earth. Repentance is a necessary and salutary aspect of daily Christian living. We need it as much in our ongoing pilgrimage as we did at our initial conversion. For no tokenistic reason did our Lord label John the greatest. He had such a high and holy, important and preparatory work to do; there can be no faith without repentance, just as no repentance without faith—the two go hand in hand.

If we were forgiven and then just left to make our way to heaven through our own righteousness, what an impossible and discouraging feat it would be. But we are to turn *from* the alluring, tempting, powerful false gods of this doomed world *to* Someone infinitely better. John's was no joyless and impossible task but an epic relief for the whole of humanity; to the Jew first but rapidly to the Gentile world. Christ's substituting atonement for us on the Cross was nigh.

UNPALATABLE TRUTHS

John was not only to be another Samson, another Samuel but also another Elijah. As the original Elijah strove to awaken the Jews to the greatness and supremacy of the true God, so John, the Bridegroom's best man, was to "go before him" with the goal of bringing about a mighty awakening, a great returning, a national revival.

Unlike Christ whose conversations with Samaritans, Romans, lepers, tax-collectors and immoral women were recorded for our benefit, John's peculiar, preparatory mission was to reach these ethnic Jews. They were the ones since the time of the patriarchs who had gradually been going astray. They were the ones who would be the first to hear the good news inscribed in John's name—'God is gracious'. They were the ones who were to be returned to the fundamentals of their faith, in which God had called a people in spirit and truth on pilgrimage to a heavenly, promised land.

The last few verses of the final prophet Malachi were thus repeated to reiterate the momentousness of the new order, known to us as the Gospel age. Just as the wilderness wanderings of Israel ended up blessing the younger rather than older generation of Jews of that time, the age of Gospel proclamation would be an unspeakable blessing to multitudes of younger Jews and thenceforth Gentiles through the ages. John's own father, Zacharias for example, we assume, would be deeply moved by his son's preaching—not the other way round.

The "hearts" of the older generation were to be pricked, convicted of sin, born again, or would perish in the wilderness of outward religion. As with race, place, face, even national grace, the elderly can be as proud if not prouder than the young. Along with all preachers and pastors down the ages, John the Baptist would do what every faithful one of them has done—preach Christ, point to Christ, prioritize Christ. If you have Him, you have eternal life. If not, damnation.

These are hard truths on which souls have choked, stumbled, and fallen. They can be unpalatable and hateful to the naturally proud peacock flesh. Preaching is a twofold job, which locks in on Christ, believing that in Him is all recompense, all refuge, all relief. There is the job of destroying the false premise that the self can please God or enter heaven by anything it is or does. Then, there is the job of re-constituting the self in God's image; re-setting, re-building, re-making it in Christ.

Without doubt, John would have bypassed all the externals of outward religion and gone straight for the jugular of the moral law. All other laws, when boiled down, come down to (a) do you love God? (b) do you love God's image—man?

John would have striven by grace to open the ears of his hearers, convincing them in the power of the Holy Spirit that their lives were answering 'No' to both (a) or (b), and so they desperately needed (c)—CHRIST.

How close He was to him; how close are we to Him.

But are you IN Him; is He IN you?

What or who is Christ to you?

7

Blessings and rebukes

> "And Zacharias said unto the angel, Whereby shall I know this? For I am an old man, and my wife well stricken in years. And the angel answering said unto him, I am Gabriel, that stands in the presence of God; and am sent to speak unto thee, and to show thee these glad tidings. And, behold, thou shalt be dumb, and not able to speak, until the day that these things shall be performed, because thou believest not my words, which shall be fulfilled in their season" (Luke 1:18–20).

AS SO OFTEN IN Scripture, we are tempted to look down on and judge another, without realizing that we would most likely be in the same boat or worse. True it is that Zacharias didn't exemplify the faith of a Hannah or an Abraham of yore; yet equally true that we moderns have the fulfilled, completed word of God in our hands and yet esteem it too lightly, not believing many of its promises *in practice*. We have no moral high ground from which to censure Zacharias, seeing as we have far greater blessings and clearer knowledge, living in the Gospel age with many commentaries, biographies and sermons at our disposal.

There is another sense, though, in which this father-son pair; Zacharias (*God remembers*) and John (*God is gracious*), represent the handing over of the baton from the Old (concealed) to New (revealed) Testament age, fulfilling that last verse of Malachi 4:6 in which the hearts of patriarchal Old Testament parents and their New Testament progeny would be mutually enlivened and edified: "And he" (that is, John the Baptist) "shall turn the heart of the fathers to the children, and the heart of the children to their fathers, lest I come and smite the earth with a curse." New Testament believers are to love the Old Testament, just as those living in the time of Christ should have embraced and rejoiced in His coming, and welcomed those barren Gentiles into God's fructifying kingdom.

The whole of the Old Testament age from Abraham to John the Baptist would be subsumed in the infinitely better age of the New, fulfilled in Christ. In such an outward, ceremonial form of true religion, we might sympathize with Zacharias' slowness in fully comprehending what the angel meant re the immediate promise and the 'forerunner', spiritual-Elijah status his son would embody. The man had faith and yet his faith was unshaped, undefined, groping in the gloom of what had been held in shadows, types and pictures for millennia.

The whole religion of outward Judaism was ripe and had run its course. Thousands of sacrifices had been offered up for thousands of years; hundreds of thousands, perhaps millions of believers by faith had rested their souls on Messiah from afar but had died not having apprehended the royal Seed, looking to the first and second coming of Messiah as at two distant mountain peaks which seemed as one. John's parents were aged, weary, subject to the aches and pains of mortality, living in the final days of Old Testament religion, clinging on by faith but, understandably, struggling to apprehend the extent of the glory which would soon come.

We are similarly jaded and weary as we look to that final mountain peak of the second coming. We also crave outward signs and lean on human reasoning; we too often allow common sense to shape our thoughts, rather than receiving God's word it as it is, thus to shape our lives in response to its authority, seeing as it is not a collection of cunningly devised tales but the very word of God.

Do we, in this Gospel age, who pray for revival in the land, really believe it will come? We strive to be a blessing to the local church, a good witness in the workplace, but do we genuinely apprehend the eye of God upon us, looking not only at everything we do and say, but at everything that passes through our minds?

A NEW BAND

Unlike the weary *old man* of the Old Testament, the *new man* of the New Testament has good news of the risen Savior to impart to a benighted, dead world. Every AD believer is equipped to answer every sinner with good news. We no longer anticipate the Messiah to come but rejoice in the Messiah who has come, has seen, has conquered.

Gabriel, moreover, whose name means *mighty one of God*, typifies the believer, mighty in Christ who is their strength. Believers stand in the presence of God because they stand by faith upon His Word, with the Spirit to guide them. Believers are not sent to fearfully debate or subtly argue with clever minds but are "sent" to declare, to proclaim, to "speak" the things which have been commissioned by the King.

New Testament believers are privileged to live in the time of Incarnation, after the time when Immanuel deigned to descend and dwell in our midst, walking among us in the flesh. He would permit Himself to be born as a baby, dandled and cooed over; to grow up as a typical human yet without sin, thence to identify with us and die in our stead.

Gabriel points to a new band of believers which is no longer bound by types, pictures and shadows but lives "to show" men and women what the Lord Jesus has done for them. We may point not only to future but to past glory, for in history Christ has done in deed what He said He would do in Genesis 3 when the Seed was first prophesied. That most majestic of chapters, Hebrews 11, reminds us that all those Old Testament saints were not privileged to receive what we New Testament believers have. And so, as Malachi

4:6 commands, we are to love our Old Testament forebears who were looking by faith to Christ.

The people of God, from John's time onward, would no longer be restricted to one geographical area known as Israel, for the tent pegs would burst free and take on the breadth of the planet, entitling the likes of us to enter the Holy of holies through Christ our Prophet, Priest and King who went before us. New Testament children who once walked in the spiritually dark parts of the planet, and our Old Testament forebears who were privileged to have the Scriptures revealed to them may rejoice together—Jews and Gentiles united by faith in the promised Seed. In Him we find everything worth living for and we cannot restrain our joy or remain silent as Zacharias was forced to for a season:

"Sing, O barren, thou *that* didst not bear; break forth into singing, and cry aloud, thou *that* didst not travail with child: for more *are* the children of the desolate than the children of the married wife, saith the LORD. Enlarge the place of thy tent, and let them stretch forth the curtains of thine habitations: spare not, lengthen thy cords, and strengthen thy stakes; for thou shalt break forth on the right hand and on the left; and thy seed shall inherit the Gentiles, and make the desolate cities to be inhabited." (Isa 54:1–3)

HAMPERED BY UNBELIEF

The world's legal system is concerned primarily with physical actions proven to have been committed. God's system of justice is far higher; reviewing not only the actions but the thoughts and the words committed *and* omitted which ought not to have been omitted. Zacharias merely spoke a few words based on a few thoughts, and yet it warranted the chastisement of temporary dumbness. We must confess, sadly, that there are times when dumbness would be a blessing, for we are prone to go astray, say the wrong thing, allow our thoughts to stray into unprofitable pastures.

The burden of words and thoughts is often too much for us, for in our weakness and instability we are not as godly-minded and spiritually salty as we would like. A season of quietness and meditation can be more blessing than curse; Zacharias would have the providential chance of living up to his name more fully; to be a prayerful *rememberer* of God, remembering the extent to which God had remembered him.

As with all chastisements for believers, they are temporary and spiritually salutary. Zacharias would be able to speak again; his dumbness only endured "until the day" that John the best man, the forerunner of Christ, was born. We would be benefitted, spiritually, if we were a little more loosened to the things of this world, for they are passing and will one day dissolve into glory.

Zacharias' dumbness reminds us of our own impotence to think right and say right, let alone do righteousness in God's sight. His standard is so far above ours that we must be rendered passively receptive before His blessing is granted. Like Zacharias, we are often hampered by unbelief—not the unbeliever's unbelief of rebellion and deadness but the believer's unbelief of weariness and waywardness. We may be men and women of faith yet it takes a lifetime for our faith to grow, to become stronger, more trusting, more obedient, more sincere, more yielded, yearly, monthly, daily, hourly, minutely.

Our faith is like a flickering candle which, when compared with Christ's light in us, seems invisible. Nevertheless, if we have faith we rejoice; if we have faith we know that all is well with our souls. The Lord, as with Zacharias, shall fulfill His purpose through us. All births point us to the ultimate Birth of Christ. He was born once, so that through Him we could be born from above. He died in judgment and wrath once, that we might not experience it at all.

WHETHER WE MARVEL

> "And the people waited for Zacharias, and marveled that he tarried so long in the temple. And when he came out, he could not speak unto them: and they perceived that he had seen a vision in the temple: for he beckoned unto them, and remained speechless" (Luke 1:21–22).

The people were waiting for Zacharias; some hungry and thirsty for personal forgiveness and communion, others to complete their customary ceremonial rite which would culminate in the Aaronic benediction: "The LORD bless thee, and keep thee: the LORD make his face shine upon thee, and be gracious unto thee: the LORD lift up his countenance upon thee, and give thee peace." (Num 6:24-26). The process itself shouldn't have lasted for more than an hour; the great scholar and Jewish convert, Alfred Edersheim, describes it thus:

"Before him—somewhat farther away, towards the heavy Veil that hung before the Holy of Holies, was the golden altar of incense, on which the red coals glowed. To his right (the left of the altar—that is, on the north side) was the table of shewbread; to his left, on the right or south side of the altar, was the golden candlestick. And still he waited, as instructed to do, till a special signal indicated, that the moment had come to spread the incense on the altar, as near as possible to the Holy of Holies. Priests and people had reverently withdrawn from the neighborhood of the altar, and were prostrate before the Lord, offering unspoken worship, in which record of past deliverance, longing for mercies promised in the future, and entreaty for present blessing and peace, seemed the ingredients of the incense, that rose in a fragrant cloud of praise and prayer. Deep silence had fallen on the worshippers, as if they watched to heaven the prayers of Israel, ascending in the cloud of odors' that rose from the golden altar in the Holy Place. Zacharias waited, until he saw the incense kindling. Then he also would have bowed down in worship, and reverently withdrawn, had not a wondrous sight arrested his steps." (from the must-read *The Life and Times of Jesus the Messiah*).

As the people waited and waited, we must compare ourselves with them; for if a preacher goes on for more than his allotted 40 minutes, how quick we are to look at the time rather than become lost in wonder at the enormity of the things God is preaching through him. It is right and proper that we pay close attention to the words of a faithful minister of the word of God; more important that we crave not just the explanations and applications of the word but the God of the word—the Triune Godhead being the true fundament and focus of all acceptable worship; implicitly if not always explicitly.

The question is not whether we marvel at any slight change in the pulpit or order of service, or striking illustrations and insights given to us for our good. The primary question is how much we marvel at the God of the universe after our religious activities are over. How much do we marvel at the creation of the Creator; how deeply do we marvel at God's dealings with us? How adoringly and affirmingly do we look up and marvel at our God? How long do these things stay with us during Monday to Saturday, anchored and re-fueled as these six days should be in the Love of our lives, more fully meditated on during Sunday worship, one day in seven, but resorted to day by day as a matter of conscious, joyful habit?

Religiousness, although time-consuming, is relatively easy because it can be compartmentalized and put in a box. Godliness is our core challenge and is relatively rare because it must touch every part of our lives, from the moment we wake up to the moment we sleep, 24–7, 365.

SILENCE SPEAKS

Our tongues can be as much a blessing as a curse, for a tongue is a thing which can empower and enliven a once-dead soul; sadly, it is most often used by the world to ensnare and exalt human ego, leading dead souls further onward in sin.

Zacharias "could not speak" at this moment but, if he could have, would he have wanted to? Could he have done justice to the glory and unfathomable holiness which he had witnessed, or to the sense of embarrassment and contrition he had experienced due to his own unbelief? Sometimes we would do better not to speak at all, but rather to commit ourselves to silent meditation. Sometimes our silence speaks more powerfully than our muddled words. Often we find we have ended up saying too much or too little, or not in a way that is honoring to our Father. It is no bad thing, therefore, to speak a little less and think a little more before we lock and load that most potent of weapons—tongue.

Equally, the people "perceived" something at this point. They were keen to perceive spiritual things, desirous of receiving blessing, tending to those things which had to do with the eternal rather than the temporal. We do well when we tune our vision to the things which are to do with the Lord. The older we get the more we should be remembering how brief a time we have on earth; roughly three score and ten; a third of that spent asleep, another third in necessary bodily concerns; amid many distractions, do we set aside the appropriate amount of time each day on the *all things* of 1 Corinthians 3:21: "Therefore let no man glory in men. For all things are yours"?

We read in 1 Corinthians 1:22 that "the Jews require a sign" and here the Lord was pleased to grant them one in the form of "a vision." We may consider what exactly Zacharias did by his having "beckoned." Every preacher worth his salt will agree that the best thing he can do is to beckon minds *to* Christ and *from* self. The best of preachers focus on Christ and will avoid histrionics or showmanship in the pulpit. Just as the brazen serpent required not learning or education but a look, humans can be saved by a look; so long as they look by faith to the Savior and not anywhere else. Lives are looking in all sorts of places. As for you, in your life, where are you looking?

Zacharias "remained speechless," although nothing is revealed to us about how he felt. Perhaps Zacharias was relieved from the burden of having to make sense of things in a way that his curious and inquisitive brethren would expect; relieved from having to articulate and express something of the glory which had been revealed to him, and from being tempted to explain away his own painful unbelief, allowing him an appropriate time for self-examination and repentance. There is "a time to keep silence, and a time to speak," as that profound and beautiful chapter 3 of Ecclesiastes proclaims.

MORE A TYPE OF CHRIST

"And it came to pass, that, as soon as the days of his ministration were accomplished, he departed to his own house. And after those days his wife Elisabeth conceived, and hid herself five months, saying, thus hath the Lord dealt with me in the days wherein he looked on *me*, to take away my reproach among men." (Luke 1:23–25).

What consternation, tumult and joy must have been in this beloved priest's head during this momentous but short period of time. Struck dumb and quite possibly deaf due to unbelief, yet assured of the most wonderful promises; encountered by an angel; promised a son; that son the forerunner of Messiah. Who could take it in. How much he would have wanted to return to the joyful embrace of his delighted wife, to the calm domesticity of his own home and yet for these days he was obliged to complete his ordained "ministration." All things have their time and Zacharias was not one to do things according to his own will. There would be the proper time for him to return home and escape the many quizzical faces which could not fathom his various inward musings.

Life is not such a long affair, after all. After we have completed those earthly tasks to which we have been appointed, it is time for us to depart and go our heavenly way. Maybe Zacharias was permitted to meditate not only on the short-term, joyful and amazing events about to occur, but on the heavenly realm in which he now surely dwells. We each have a set number of days and this earth in its present state is not our home.

Had Zacharias not been rendered dumb, what rash and ill-considered words might he have uttered; what gushing, unmeasured praise and personal delight might he have expressed; his inward meditations and holy ruminations would have evaporated. Indeed, his silent state would endure throughout the pregnancy of his dear wife, Elisabeth. There would be the right time for all manner of praise and thanksgiving at the end of it, but for now he would be temporarily held hostage by his own mind, ministering to his own thoughts, perhaps better able to pore over the Holy Scriptures, many of which he would have committed to memory.

We see in retrospect that the providence allotted to Zacharias made him more a type of Christ than he otherwise would have been. Rather than voluble prayers and poetical psalms offered by the tongue, his silent suffering and subsequent departure to "his own house" mysteriously pointed to his, our, Lord and Savior. The God-man was not someone given to excessive words or long conversations. He was a man of few words but those words are worth more than all of the words of the world combined.

Moreover, "after those days" when Christ's infinitely superior, perfect ministrations were accomplished, He would ascend back to His heavenly home in glory, there to oversee the salvation of each elect soul from physical to spiritual birth; thence to glory. Hence, Zacharias' silence and patience mirrors the life of the Priest of priests.

Likewise, Zacharias' biological son, the best man, would rejoice not in the power or longevity of his own words or life but in ministering to the Jewish people as their final prophet who would, as it were, have a foot in both Old and New Testament camps. He would point *away from* self and *to* Christ whose fourfold Incarnation-Crucifixion-Resurrection-Ascension mission accomplished what mankind could never accomplish. We can get men to the moon, maybe even to Mars, but not even one soul to heaven. It is beyond us.

HE LOOKED ON

There is so much that is condensed in Scripture, "those days" being an example. What delight and joy existed between those two believers who basked in the promise given—the husband communing silently with the wife. What prayer, thanksgiving, amazement and awe would have been in that household during "those days," intensified when those first signs of conception and pregnancy appeared.

"Elisabeth conceived," we are told, and we too must perceive Christ in the Scriptures; find Him gloriously there, more so than in the heavenly night skies or mysterious oceanic depths. God delights in being conceived of in His word, His most complete revelation. When we first conceive of the deity of Christ, what amazement there is. When the Word speaks to us personally, reading us and defining us in ways which are unerringly true, how awed we are, how willing to rejoice in the word of God, and in the God of the word.

The number "five" bespeaks grace and goodness, according to many wise exegetes. No matter how good our personal news and inward experiences, the ultimate good news is to await the One through whom all things came. The *sixth* month would mark that transitional point in which the Holy Spirit points from John to Jesus. If the miraculous conception of John in the normal course of marriage was amazing, the miraculous conception of the Son of Man would be of an altogether different sort. No earthly consummation was involved therein; no Nazarite vow or specific forerunning could apprehend this categorically different child, this otherworldly God-man.

Being a godly-minded, seasoned saint, Elisabeth sets the example, attributing her recent life events not to *her* dealings but to the Lord's dealings *with* her; all of our life's events are ultimately not attributable to us for the Lord is sovereign and does whatsoever He wills. If it had been the Lord's will to grant Elisabeth no children or a multitude of children, so it would have been. But it was the Lord's will to grant her this son at this time, to be the greatest prophet ever born. It would be the Lord's will for this son to grow up to preach repentance and faith and then go on to be beheaded for Christ's sake. Such things might not make sense to us but Elisabeth was granted the wisdom to increasingly see the Lord's hand in all; she could accept whatever unfolded as His will. Can you?

That little phrase "he looked on" refers not just to her own immediate interests and concerns but to the bigger picture of God's kingdom. When we pray, we are to pray that God's will be done on earth, whatever this might mean for us. Whether like Job or Jonah we are to descend, or like Joseph or Joshua ascend, we are to remain steady, prayerful, quiescent souls, seeking the greater glory of God's kingdom.

The Lord would soon be implementing phase 1 of His 4-step salvific operation on earth; becoming incarnate; living a perfect life on earth, dying a perfect death, being raised again to His heavenly throne. Zacharias and Elisabeth were to be used in the preface of this sacred 4-stage operation. The Lord looks upon us, yes, but no man is an island and it is of greater importance that we see ourselves as citizens of a heavenly kingdom rather than as people who have their best lives now.

Elisabeth was pleased that the "reproach" of childlessness which she had had to endure was, by God's will, now removed. A careful reading shows that it was her "reproach among men" to which she was alluding; there was no actual reproach to her soul, merely the man-centered tradition of equating barrenness with curse, fertility with blessing. There have been many godly women whose wombs have never been with child, just as many godless women whose wombs have birthed a brood. It is not necessarily a blessing or a curse, either way. If Elisabeth had never conceived it would have been fine by her, for she had her Beloved.

The God-man

8

A highly favored virgin

> "And in the sixth month the angel Gabriel was sent from God unto a city of Galilee, named Nazareth. To a virgin espoused to a man whose name was Joseph, of the house of David; and the virgin's name was Mary."
> (Luke 1:26–27)

NUMEROLOGY CAN BE OVERLY fixated on; however, it is worth noting that, with regard to the growth of the Bridegroom's best man, John, *five* months is mentioned in verse 24, whereas here the "sixth month" is emphasized in verse 26.

Thinking back to the original *sixth* day, we recall how all of creation was for man, not man for it; the outpouring of God into this special creature, His image-bearer, was magnificent, representing the pinnacle of His six days of creation. This made the subsequent rebellion and fall that much more tragic and momentous, for there was a sense in which man lost his humanity during that existential crisis; a sense in which man's spiritual relationship with God came to an end; in which man from thence would have "no preeminence above a beast" (Eccl 3:19) and would be "like the beasts that perish" (Ps 49:20).

In other words, man *could not* live up to the role which had been assigned him at creation and *would not* fulfill the responsibilities and expectations which came with that sixth day. In Adam, we utterly and irrevocably failed, and so a new Adam, a second Adam, a last Adam, a spiritual Adam was desperately required. Thank the Lord, the ruined human race would in time have this Adam to Whom to look and by faith live, for "the first man *is* of the earth, earthy: the second man *is* the Lord from heaven." (1 Cor 15:47)

Individual testimonies will often reveal a person, a ruined sinner, brought to the point of failure, realization of brokenness and failure before anything spiritually reconstructive would, by grace, occur. Mankind has been being prepared through the centuries, thank God, for this only remedy for our common Fall. Those glorious middle chapters of Isaiah, in this regard, majestically command us to "Comfort ye, comfort ye" (Isa 40:1), "Keep silence before me" (Isa 41:1), "Behold my servant" (Isa 42:1).

There would be a man to come into this universe who was truly a man in every sense, except for sin. This servant alone would be able and willing to represent us. He would be "the last Adam" (1 Cor 15:45) who would live on earth as Adam (we) ought to have lived in order to fulfill our high calling upon earth. He would be accepted in and of Himself because He was God the Son and the Son of Man who "learned he obedience by the things which he suffered" (Heb 5:8). He was "in the form of God" (Phil 2:6) yet "took upon him the form of a servant" (2:7), being "found in fashion as a man" (2:8).

Ironically, at this point He would still have been in heaven and would not yet have made that stupendous journey of infinite descent which would mark the first of His humiliations; the initial humiliation of dwelling in the body of a creature although Creator. The angel Gabriel was sent by God—Father, Son, Holy Spirit. Son was not *yet* Immanuel in that sense of being conceived in the womb, for the Holy Spirit would soon hover over that chosen human womb.

The mission of salvation through Incarnation was not yet activated at this point. Nevertheless, God's plan, if we correctly read Isaiah, would see it come; this tiny speck of perfect humanity the supreme Servant of this fallen human race: "Behold my servant, whom I uphold; mine elect, *in whom* my soul delighteth; I have put my spirit upon him: he shall bring forth judgment to the Gentiles." (Isa 42:1).

If we rightly read the literal Cyrus (in Isaiah) as the typified Christ, this brief, earthly, spiritual mission would be such that, after the descension from heaven into the virgin's womb, this tiny babe in the manger would within a relatively short lifespan conquer death for millions, then rise as mighty Conqueror-Savior, then reign gloriously over all parts of the planet: "I have raised up one from the north, and he shall come: from the rising of the sun shall he call upon my name: and he shall come upon princes as *upon* morter, and as the potter treadeth clay." (Isa 41:25) He was both "north" of the human race in terms of being infinitely outside of us in Divinity; yet "south" in terms of sharing our humanity here with us, sans sin.

All the while, the Second Person of the Godhead was aloft, on the heavenly throne, looking earthward as one who "sitteth upon the circle of the earth" (Isa 40:22). Interestingly, "Galilee," etymologically, has to do with encircling or rolling, for Christ is indeed the circumference of His creation; in Him we have our being. The Incarnation was soon to be activated within the womb; even then, this would not be exactly the same as being out here on earth with the rest of us, shoulder to shoulder. Soon He would dwell within our human radius, cheek by jowl.

He who had stretched "out the heavens a curtain" (Isa 40:22) was about to travel a dizzyingly, mind-bogglingly vast distance to take up His stay of residence within "Nazareth," the root of that city's name having to do with watching and scattering. He, the God-man, in His Incarnation would be an enigma, a riddle, a paradox, a stumbling-block, an infuriation to the unbelieving and disobedient whose stubborn wills would "not be planted," "not be sown," "not take root in the earth" (Isa 40:24)—fallen man, all of us in Adam, will always believe the lie that we own the earth and everything in it.

But Salvation is of the LORD.

THE BEST MAN AWAITS

Despite the sense of *apparent* frailty and vulnerability to which the Lord would willingly submit, even as a baby in a feeding-trough designed for beasts, unrecognized by this vain, self-aggrandizing world, with "no beauty that we should desire him" (Isa 53:2), nevertheless here, shortly before Him was one being raised up as a forerunner who would be the best man, "the voice of him that crieth in the wilderness" (Isa 40:3) who would announce the coming of the perfect and representative man who alone could fulfill the promise of the sixth day.

John the Baptizer would have a glorious job to do in the short time he was granted breath upon earth. He would be privileged to announce the disruption of the space-time continuum by the Holy One through Whom it was created. He would be honored with the first Anno Domini gospel call to mankind in which salvation would be through the Christ who would live among us, to be offered up for us. There is no human philosophy or art which can rival what the Scriptures say about this, as we have already seen in the first part of Isaiah 40; John's preaching might well be outlined in the whole of Isaiah 40–52 which precedes the next step in the four-fold mission—The Crucifixion.

On Mary's name we may meditate a little. Linked etymologically to *Mariam* and *Miriam*, it most likely has connotations of bitterness or rebellion, which might come as a surprise to some. Mary, of course, has been idolized to ruinous effect by centuries of Roman Catholic pomp and circumstance.

It is useful to connect Mary to first woman, Eve, through whom we all have come. Through Eve we have our physical, earthly existences of flesh and blood which cannot inherit the kingdom of God. No wonder the name Mary carries such negative weight, then, for woman since the time of the Fall has been under a greater sense of difficulty and labor in childbirth; more dependent on Adam than was the case originally.

Thus, an intervention was necessary, an irruption into this natural, cursed trajectory of fallen humanity. Before their espousal was consummated, for in those days it could be some time between betrothal and wedding, this faithful Joseph ('Increaser', 'Repeater', 'Doubler') and this believing yet burdened Mary who would later bear baby James, Joses, Simon, Judas and a number of daughters, would like every Jewish woman have had the promise of the Seed somewhere in the recesses of her mind. However, never would she have presumptuously believed *she* would be the one chosen before time to have *her* life's course most wonderfully altered, and the bitterness of mankind whose flesh is as grass forever uplifted through the long-awaited Seed Incarnate.

Mary was unique in that the One who would redeem her would supernaturally be conceived within her. Her salvation, like ours, still depended on what this Holy One would do on the Cross. If the Lord of heaven had not chosen and prepared this woman through whom to enter earth and become Incarnate, we would still to this day be dwelling in our earthly tabernacles, having no hope of eternal life, no notion of being spiritually translated.

The baby that would be born miraculously within the womb of this "virgin" would, without doubt or irony be qualified and enabled to say to this woman and us, "I, *even* I, *am* the LORD; and beside me *there is* no savior" (Isa 43:11). Even as a twelve-year old, he would say with holy sincerity and solemn reverence to His earthly guardians, "How is it that ye sought me? wist ye not that I must be about my Father's business?' (Luke 2:49).

The honor and glory which God has bestowed upon a woman reminds us how much the Lord values and esteems both man and woman—together the image of God: "So God created man in his *own* image, in the image of God created he him; male and female created he them" (Gen 1:27). One ought not to be raised up to the detriment of the other, for both are the image of God. False religions will over-esteem the worth of man or the worth of woman, and so skew the divine balance.

9

The news foretold

> "And the angel came in unto her, and said, Hail, *thou that art* highly favoured, the Lord *is* with thee: blessed *art* thou among women. And when she saw *him*, she was troubled at his saying, and cast in her mind what manner of salutation this should be. And the angel said unto her, Fear not, Mary: for thou hast found favour with God. And, behold, thou shalt conceive in thy womb, and bring forth a son, and shalt call his name JESUS. He shall be great, and shall be called the Son of the Highest: and the Lord God shall give unto him the throne of his father David: And he shall reign over the house of Jacob for ever; and of his kingdom there shall be no end." (Luke 1:28–33)

IN HER SOUL, MARY experienced the joy of sins forgiven, repentance granted, a life lived by faith. In her body she was set apart, her womb the entrance-point for God the Son to be born in the flesh so as to represent and redeem us from the curse of the Fall. Crucially, it was not this bodily responsibility and privilege which saved her; like anyone saved who is saved, she was saved by grace not works. This most unique and amazing work of carrying the Seed to full term and being the mother of Jesus earned her nothing in terms of salvation.

Like every other sinner saved, the due process of the moral law was to be fulfilled *for* her so that salvation would be complete. Other than the unique, miraculous conception and physical birth, we may spiritually apply the "highly favored," "the Lord *is* with thee," and the "blessed *art* thou" to our own souls, if we are of the household of faith. We are each a miraculous work of sovereign grace.

In a sense, it is more blessed to have the miraculous gift of faith than to give birth to the Promised Seed, as the adult Jesus will later explain with mild rebuke: "And it came to pass, as he spake these things, a certain woman of the company lifted up her voice, and said unto him, Blessed *is* the womb that bare thee, and the paps which thou hast sucked. But he said, Yea rather, blessed *are* they that hear the word of God, and keep it." (Luke 11:27–28). The priority of spiritual faith remains paramount.

We may rightly marvel, nevertheless, at the uniqueness and peculiarity of Mary's calling—she was prepared from eternity to be the woman through whom the God-man would emerge incarnate, to dwell with us and substitute Himself for us. From nothing, we who were made in His image were granted everything. Yet, having everything, we foolishly chose the nothingness of pride and rebellion over the everything of gratitude and heartfelt obedience to our Heavenly Father. His love for us is beyond comprehension.

The subsequent journey of human history has been one of mercy upon mercy, blessing after blessing—the Seed promise granted to first man and woman, the salvation of Noah from the Flood, the calling out of Moses with a vast multitude, the institution of a godly king and holy temple in a promised land, etc. etc. From God's purview, this journey has been one of longsuffering, love and a willingness to descend and sacrifice for us, the ungodly and unholy; nowhere more greatly shown than in the Incarnation and Crucifixion.

Even in the depths of our pride and rebellion, God the Son stooped to become as one of us, conceived in the womb of a nobody from nowhere, taking upon Him the humiliation of flesh and blood rather than letting us receive the damnation we deserve.

Our Creator would not remain infinitely aloof but would take decisive and miraculous action in time, intervening thus to do what none else could or would—dwelling as a human in righteousness rather than rebellion; wearing the fallen, pitiable garb of the sinner whilst remaining sinless; walking like a moribund creature subject to infirmity whilst being eternal Creator.

A giant becoming a dwarf or man becoming a worm are unfit analogies to illustrate this, but they may vaguely hint at something of the depths to which our beloved Savior would descend so as to be "with" us.

WHY ME?

The vision "she saw" was not as troubling as the "saying" of God, for human Mary, like us, was a fallen child of Adam saved by grace. If she had been some higher being; a mediatrix, as the church of Rome still claims in its catechism, there would have been no reference to her being "troubled" or having ruminated about such things "in her mind," examining them from different angles, applying them to her personal life, wondering about how it all might be worked out.

Her espoused one, Joseph, meanwhile, would be severely tested so that angelic assistance was needed. Her responsibility would be of the highest known to mankind since the days of Adam and Eve. Who is sufficient for such things and who, but by grace, could be so favored and blessed as to accept these things without pride puffing up.

So it is with the born again. To be washed of all sin and granted a place in heaven is at first so overwhelming. Speaking from personal experience, I can remember wondering *Why me?* and *What next?* I recall handing out tracts in an underground train station in London during that first flush of Christian living, wondering where it was all heading, considering JESUS and earnestly desiring that others would also be granted the personal knowledge of Him. They simply had to read God's word, I naïvely thought, and they would automatically be born again.

The warfare of the Christian life, we find, is one of constant, relentless mental warfare, the thought-life a battleground which doesn't ease with age. Emotions, feelings, intimations come and go, but the sheer quantity of thoughts that pass through your head at any given time of day or night is stupendous—so much to be processed as we endeavor to make good on those promises and new life miraculously granted. Pride ever lurks.

The "salutation" of God is irrevocable—once saved always saved. Even so, we fear displeasing God more each day, knowing what terrible ingratitude and disobedience we can fall into if we take our eyes off Christ. Mary was, like us, called by faith to work out her own salvation with fear and trembling. Despite being granted such closeness to Christ in the flesh, she was still dependent on the spiritual apprehension of Him for the sustenance of her soul. She could found her assurance on the "salutation" made to her, not on her efforts to be godly.

FEAR NOT

There is ungodly fear and godly fear, the latter being healthy for the soul, the former ruinous. The former turns people away from serious contemplation of life and death, dooming them to remain branded in hell-bound herd. At best, they may even adopt the appearance of true religion, all the while trampling on the pages of Scripture and despising their sin's solution—JESUS—deeming His Cross-work barbaric, antiquated, impotent. The fear of the ungodly is a negative fear of loss: health, possessions, pleasures, opportunities, friendships, successes, recognitions and awards.

The fear of the godly, by compare, is the positive fear of God's holiness; an awareness of the utter unfitness and uncleanness of the fallen creature à propos the holy Creator who is all righteous, pure, perfect, omnipotent, omniscient, omnipresent. How, think the godly, can I come before Him knowing what I know about myself, knowing He knows me as I really am.

Mary, if she *were* to be called the Immaculate Virgin or Mediatrix co-equal with Christ, which she shouldn't, would have no truck with either form of fear. She would not be in a position of abhorring her sins and looking up with reverence and awe towards God. The travesty of this false view of her, sadly propagated by the Church of Rome, High Church of England and others, is that it disconnects Mary from us for Mary like us was a saved-sinner. Like all the saints, she was one who depended for her salvation on the life, death and resurrection of her Savior.

She struggled with her old nature, as do we. She trod along the narrow way, repenting of her sins daily, renewing her faith by looking to its Author. She had godly fear and yet, like us, was commanded to "Fear not," to strive with all her heart to obey. The challenge to fear not would guide her, as the promises and exhortations of God uplift us. When we read of commands such as 'Fear not' and in other places 'Rejoice', we are to take them seriously. If we give in to ungodly fear and do not rejoice, this is to disobey.

We are to "Fear not" because, like Mary, in spite of our stubborn, strong and bitter 'Mara' roots, we have "found favor with God." We do not know why; why us and not our neighbor; why us and not our friend; why us and not our colleague; why us and not our blood relation. We pray for them but rejoice within for we have found something of eternal value.

We compare Scripture with Scripture and realize that, in a greater sense, we were found by rather than found God; sought by rather than sought. If He hadn't intervened in our lives according to His perfect will, we never would have found Him.

NEW BIRTH

There is much mystery surrounding conception, even in our day of technological know-how. Some "conceive" easily while others do not, even with all manner of modern medical expertise being applied. If the wonder of regular conception is one thing, the wonder of God being conceived in human flesh and dwelling among us is altogether *other*.

The uniqueness of the Incarnation is rightly wondered at for all sorts of theological reasons. Yet, it is also important not to lose sight of the absolute necessity that we, each, as individuals, receive JESUS in our souls; for we may admire Him from afar and still go to hell!

As a race, we have from the beginning turned to the darkness, listened to the voices of rebellion and ingratitude, wasted our potential and labored to bring forth fruitless works. Nevertheless, millions would "conceive" through the centuries, from Abel and Enoch all the way to the international church of the 21st century. Many rebellious, ungrateful hearts would be broken and made ready to receive JESUS within. He alone lived the perfect life—we cling on for dear life to His dear life.

Are you born again? When was it that you went from being of the flesh to being of the Spirit? You may be someone for whom the second birth has not occurred; one who wrestles with a strong sense of doubt over your spiritual birth. Simply speaking, you must receive Christ and become a child of God, for "as many as received him, to them gave he power to become the sons of God, *even* to them that believe on his name" (John 1:12). If you are not a child of God, you are not heading for an eternity with your Heavenly Father—you have no such Father.

We are told in other parts of Scripture of the "day star" which, for those who take heed, will "arise in" their dark "hearts" (2 Pet 1:19). The apostle Paul, after his own spiritual birth "in Christ," rejoiced at having "begotten you through the gospel" (1 Cor 4:15). Galatians 4:19 reveals the necessity of "Christ" being "formed in" us.

If you do not have Christ in you, "the eyes of your understanding" have not yet been "enlightened" (Eph 1:18)—you have not been born again and you remain in your sins.

THE UNIQUE AND SPECIAL MAN

The first thing that might puzzle us here is how God manifest in the flesh could "be great," future tense, seeing as He is great. We may also be perplexed by Christ being called, future tense, "the Son of the Highest," given that He is ever the Second Person of the

Trinity. How could David be "his father," for through God the Son all things came.

These and other questions are connected with the Incarnation, for that was the unrepeatable miracle, the coming of the perfect Man, visibly proving Himself in God's and man's sight to be morally perfect. He lived an exemplary, sinless life unlike another. His greatness was, in a sense, earned, in that the first man Adam could have obeyed God's law and merited eternal life ("And the LORD God commanded the man, saying, Of every tree of the garden thou mayest freely eat" Gen 2:16), but of his own free will he (we in him) rebelled.

In another sense, it wasn't enough for Christ to have been the One through whom creation came, for His greatness had a still higher goal, that is, the substitutionary atonement for rebel Adam's ruined race. Even unbelievers would feel compelled to call him righteous and Son of God at Calvary, such was the uniqueness and specialness of Him.

We who lay claim to know something of His greatness and deity are effectively living off His royalties, so to speak; His righteousness being credited to our account. He the Author, we the recipients of His salvific magnus opus. Scripture tells us that He as God will give us a place on His throne, just as He as Man earned the right to sit upon it through His earthly, incarnate, righteous life.

Although we read of Him prayerfully communing with God the Father when on earth, we never read of Him repenting, for He had no need. To repent implies having sinned; if He had sinned just once then His earthly righteousness would have been sullied; like us, He would have been a law-breaker.

Lest we presumptuously believe we can somehow affect or bring salvation through our personal obedience and righteousness, we are reminded that He was of the Godhead, the unique and only "Son of the Highest." Lest we mystically lose ourselves in lofty meditations, our thoughts must ground themselves in His humanity, a lineage connecting Him to "his father David." David, like us, was of our fallen race, and yet it pleased God to make Him a type of Christ the King.

Jesus, like us, would be a man of flesh and blood who knew tiredness, thirst, happiness and sorrow; unlike us, would never put a foot wrong, never sin in thought, word or deed. He would exhibit absolute piety Godward; whole-hearted purity manward. He would know not even one moment of covetousness, one particle of jealousy or shred of immorality, ever.

His eyes were firmly on the prize of salvation which was of Him and which He was willing to win for us, shedding His blood and permitting His beard to be spitefully pulled, His body to be broken, that wretches like us may be made whole. Because we could not, cannot, would not, will not come to Him, He could and can and would and will come to us, for "I bring near my righteousness; it shall not be far off, and my salvation shall not tarry: and I will place salvation in Zion for Israel my glory." (Isa 46:13).

He has righteousness enough for a wretched sinner like you.

HIS KINGDOM

Similarities and differences abound; we have kingdoms, spheres of influence, empires in this world. None has lasted or will; our leaders lie in mausoleums or stand in cold metallic statues. Their reigns have often been brief, bloody and brutal, their personal relationships treacherous and fraught.

So different the reign of our Savior, Jesus Christ. His yoke is mild; to serve Him is a privilege not a chore, an honor not a pain. "He shall reign" yes, but we will serve willingly and wholeheartedly because the Spirit of God has come into us; "liberty" to us "captives" has come through Him. We were "bound" but have now been released from the "prison" of sin through Him (Isa 61:1).

Because He truly is King of kings, the object of our holy affection, our servitude is unfeigned, based on love rather than fear. We are happy to play second-fiddle to Him for He was willing to lay down His earthly life for us who were opposed to Him and did "esteem him stricken, smitten of God, and afflicted" (Isa 53:4).

If Christ were to be ruler only "over the house of Jacob" according to a very literal reading, this would still be a large kingdom encompassing millions of royal subjects. However, by comparing Scripture with Scripture we are inclined to see this "house" as a type of the global church, comprising souls of every race, nation and tongue. The subjects of this universal and everlasting kingdom are not randomly but uniquely loved and eternally foreknown.

Christ came into this world of flesh and time with an agenda planned in eternity, pre Genesis 1, in which millions of specific souls would be given by God the Father to God the Son through His fourfold salvific plan: "I have manifested thy name unto the men which thou gavest me out of the world: thine they were, and thou gavest them me; and they have kept thy word" (John 17:6); each one convicted and converted through God the Spirit: "*Even the Spirit of truth; whom the world cannot receive, because it seeth him not, neither knoweth him: but ye know him; for he dwelleth with you, and shall be in you.*" (John 14:17).

Christ's "kingdom," unlike an earthly empire, is a kingdom presided over by an ageless, endless, Sovereign Savior. Once the final soul is added and Judgment Day arrives, that final number will be fixed. From that time forth there will be no further numerical addition but something altogether more glorious and wonderful; never-ending praise and worship of God Triune, redounding to eternity; ever loving, rejoicing, fellowshipping and communing; never bored, distracted, discontented, proud, or envious.

In terms of finitude and completion, this "kingdom" has no peak but will forever grow yet never conclude or reach cessation. There will be the endless exploration of the Omnipotent, Omniscient, Omnipresent, whereby our maps will never be finalized, the boundaries of our knowledge never fully discovered, new depths, heights and breadths of God endlessly enthusing and leading us into ever greater gratitude, joy with uplifted minds and hearts devoid of a single sin or prospect thereof.

10

A blessed dialogue

"And the angel answered and said unto her, The Holy Ghost shall come upon thee, and the power of the Highest shall overshadow thee: therefore also that holy thing which shall be born of thee shall be called the Son of God. And, behold, thy cousin Elisabeth, she hath also conceived a son in her old age: and this is the sixth month with her, who was called barren. For with God nothing shall be impossible. And Mary said, Behold the handmaid of the Lord; be it unto me according to thy word. And the angel departed from her." (Luke 1:34–38)

UNLIKE ZACHARIAS' RESPONSE, MARY'S contained curiosity of a more faith-filled, sanctified sort. We are told that "fear fell upon" Zacharias, implying some form of reticence or recoil from the heavy responsibility of bearing the load of such a miraculous, mighty blessing. Mary, by contrast, had godly fear but more positively "cast in her mind" for how her miraculous, epoch-changing blessing would come about. She appears to have had a more God-centered fear based on faith; Zacharias a more human-centered fear based on doubt.

No two saints are alike, of course, and in the end both reached that more consistent plane or plain of faith, by grace. In some ways, the purer and lesser tested younger believer can at times put the more battle-hardened, experienced believer to shame. To be in the world is necessarily to pick up more worldliness and, though repented of, such blemishes make it a mercy to be divinely limited to three-score and ten rather than to live for centuries, as did the saints antediluvian.

It is possible to go further and view Mary's "How shall this be . . . ?" in terms of boldness and godly mindedness, such as a zealous young person of faith from a young age might have. Mary's surprising maturity and heavenly expectation enabled her to look forward to God's wombward plan, perhaps with her godly mind recalling those well-known verses of Messianic promise in Genesis 3. Zacharias' "Whereby shall I know this?" sounds superficially similar to Mary's question, but the Lord knows the heart and could see that Zacharias was holding something back. Whom do we resemble more; Zacharias or Mary?

As we approach and experience middle to old age, we have our careers, mortgages and pensions to lose and can spend too much time feathering our nests and fretting about the secondary things, which have their right and proper place. Mary's response teaches us to lay all aside, examining and entrusting it to the Lord who will direct our steps. We do not ask enough in prayer because we do not actually want the things we should want; deep down, the cost is too great. If great blessing comes, it requires us to depend more on the Lord, trusting Him to provide the means along with the grace. The triumphs of David and riches of Solomon, we may muse, were not unqualified blessings; they carried within them the seeds of sin which needed to be mortified.

In the case of Mary, in whose womb uniquely the Incarnation would begin, the most singular and wonderful event in human history was activated. The Lord Jesus would, as planned, enter His own creation through a human mother but not earthly father. He was to be a perfect creation, untainted by the original sin imputed to Adam. He would be God and man; not half God and half man, or anything less than God or anything less than man, but fully God and fully man; the Son of God and the Son of Man, as the Athanasian Creed so helpfully describes.

His incarnation did not simply end in but was commenced in Mary's womb, for His brief three or so decades on earth *were* in effect the Incarnation in the fuller sense of the doctrine; His whole time here, with us, from manger to Cross, would be credited by grace through faith to the accounts of all those who were called to believe in Him.

Apart from sin and marriage, He would experience all the things common to man. His exemplary conduct was the prototypical life; the way each of us should have lived and should now live after spiritual conversion. Sadly and joyfully, because even after conversion we fall far short of His standard, His life on earth was substituted for our life on earth; God sees us not only as we are, but as we are in Christ; otherwise, we would soon slide into despair.

Our earthly interactions are secondary for our primary interactions are before God who sees all, just as He saw the faithful yearning of Mary who was about to experience something even greater and more unique than Adam and Eve.

MYSTERY AND MIRACLE

This dialogue, then, between the angel and Mary is yet another contrast between her and godly old Zacharias, who was beloved but chastised. God's ways are not ours; we might have expected venerable Zacharias to have had the lion's share of communion with God; young Mary to be instructed through him. The lesson for us is that those who are closer to God, more in simple prayer, more in heartfelt devotion, regular meditation and holy contemplation, will enjoy more communion with God; such believers are more ripe for communion with the Almighty who sees us as we are. There is no distinction between the inward and the outward with God; to Him they are as one.

The process of physical birth is also a picture of the spiritual conversion experience, for one's first encounter with God is a glorious and life-changing moment in which we become adopted by God and Christ is formed within us. We go from being dwellers in the flesh to dwellers in the Spirit; to having eyes filled with common sense and worldly prospects to eyes filled with spiritual wonder and eternal glimpses. Another venerable man, Nicodemus, had to be instructed in the simplest and starkest of terms that "That which is born of the flesh is flesh; and that which is born of the Spirit is spirit" (John 3:6). How many churchmen and churchwomen need to be taught the same. How many impressively robed, theologically qualified priests and vicars in our day are truly born again?

The Holy Spirit must come upon a soul before that soul can begin to have anything to do with God. Until that time, one is all flesh and prayer is nothing more than a jabbering in the dark. There is a profound sense of the mysterious and miraculous when we consider those early days of Genesis creation, when the earth was but shadowy and formless, the Spirit stirring and orchestrating it into spherical, beauteous order; similarly, an ineffable sense of mystery which surrounds human pregnancy.

But this . . . was different.

More unique and momentous than the first creation of earth and heaven and every human from Adam on, the Incarnation of God in the flesh is described as that time when "the power of the Highest shall overshadow thee." Overshadow—what human mind can begin to consider it in any other way. The cloudy and fiery pillar which followed the great exodus were but inadequate pictures of *this* overshadowing of the Almighty upon and within the womb of a lowly virgin.

It was not just the fact of the Incarnation but the cosmic implications of what it would mean for the human race. From the Fall to the Judgment, only one life has stood the test of time, has lived out the requirements of what God expects from man made in His image. The history of the human without Christ is unthinkably tragic. No redemption, no global church, no hope, no point, no end to hatred and bloodshed, and a continual tension between hearts at war with God and with each other. In a sense, Christ Jesus *is* the human race. The Godhead views us through the Second Person of the Trinity, in that all of the elect in Him were made for redemption and everlasting glorification. All things are the elect's, the Scripture reveals. John 6:65, 10:29, 15:16, and 17:6–20 can be read in no other way and should not be ignored in a mistaken attempt to ward off controversy.

Christ, the God-man was "that holy thing," for no other person, place or thing can rightly be called holy apart from "the Son of God" who took upon Himself the humiliation of human flesh. The Incarnation was the first humiliation, the stooping of Christ from His holy courts of heaven to embody the depths of human flesh so as to redeem His chosen people, being both too holy for this world and yet willing to bear its sneering disregard with perfect, divine purpose: "Thus saith the LORD, the Redeemer of Israel, *and* his Holy One, to him whom man despiseth, to him whom the nation abhorreth, to a servant of rulers, Kings shall see and arise, princes also shall worship, because of the LORD that is faithful, *and* the Holy One of Israel, and he shall choose thee" (Isa 49:7).

The Godhead had this in the Eternal Mind before earth and heaven were, and beyond the heart-breaking Fall of Man when He would no longer commune with man in that same intimate way. Christ waited with holy patience and divine pity through the times of the Flood, Tower, Patriarchs, Exodus, Israel, Tabernacle, Temple, Kings, Priests, before that awful descension from heavenly glory into earthly conception and birth. If we by grace become adopted children of God, we see Him as He rightfully is—"the Son of God"—One with the Father, One with the Spirit. One God. Three Persons. Blessèd Trinity. As we read in that useful creed:

"Furthermore it is necessary to everlasting salvation that he also believe rightly the incarnation of our Lord Jesus Christ. For the right faith is that we believe and confess that our Lord Jesus Christ, the Son of God, is God and man. God of the substance of the Father, begotten before the worlds; and man of substance of His mother, born in the world. Perfect God and perfect man, of a reasonable soul and human flesh subsisting. Equal to the Father as touching His Godhead, and inferior to the Father as touching His manhood. Who, although He is God and man, yet He is not two, but one Christ. One, not by conversion of the Godhead into flesh, but by taking of that manhood into God. One altogether, not by confusion of substance, but by unity of person. For as the reasonable soul and flesh is one man, so God and man is one Christ." (*lines 29–37 from Athanasius' 44-line Creed*)

And if we only had our sins cancelled out at Calvary, we would still not be equipped to enter heaven, without a royal robe of perfect righteousness. Christ's entire incarnate life on earth would constitute this, "For as by one man's disobedience many were made sinners, so by the obedience of one shall many be made righteous" (Rom 5:19).

While Mary would conceive her baby supernaturally, believing what the angel told her, it was unlikely she could conceive of the vast and great expanse of this "holy thing" in terms of His historical, geographical, cultural and spiritual impact on millions of fallen Adams: "But ye *are* a chosen generation, a royal priesthood, an holy nation, a peculiar people; that ye should shew forth the praises of him who hath called you out of darkness into his marvelous light" (1 Peter 2:9). With the benefit of hindsight, we are still coming to terms with who Christ is and what He has done for wretched sinners like us.

Like her, the best, safest, most honoring thing we can do is to seek to stay in His shadow throughout all our days. Better to be overshadowed by our loving heavenly Father than to let our ego soar into the stratosphere of vainglorious delusion. Praise be to God that His four-phase mission has rejuvenated and sustained this sin-sick, weary human race which started badly and will end worse. Yet for individuals, the very worst may become the best, in Him. What a plan.

JUST A 6

Mary's attention was now drawn to the work of God in the womb of her older "cousin Elisabeth," who would go on to give birth to the best man of the Bridegroom. We perhaps don't often consider enough just how great John was. Blessed from the womb, his holy, close walk with the Lord puts ours to shame. His Nazarite vow was kept to the letter, unlike Samson's. His zeal for God never dimmed with time but burned bright until its ordained end.

Like a faithful child holding a magnifying-glass, focusing the light of God upon kindling, he remained steadfast and resolute, true to his calling, never desiring attention or credit, never getting carried away with his own power, never stumbling like Hezekiah, David, Gideon, even Abraham. His was a voice crying in the wilderness and a stellar example to all subsequent souls who would claim to walk with Christ.

The name Elisabeth, to do with an oath-keeping God, reminds us that what God has intended to come to pass will come to pass. Often caught up with the news cycle, I confess the need to return to the Lord who put me on earth. He it is who guides my footsteps; He it is who wills all current events in accord with His eternal plan. Mary was to "behold" both what God was doing in her cousin's life, as well as the meaning of the name *Elisabeth*.

Mary's own name has to do with being beloved and being bitter, pointing to the necessary yet heartbreaking reality of the Cross. Elisabeth's name points to the God who has made an oath to the human race to save the multitudinous elect from the judgment from which Lucifer, fallen angels and rebellious humans will never return. In this sense, Elisabeth "in her old age" is a type of the human race in its weary, sin-sick mortality—old man Adam must die; new man Christ must live. We must die eternally or we must live eternally. For a human, there is no such thing as ceasing to be.

Here again there is reference to "the sixth month," 6 being man's number. Yes, God has our number. He knows what we are—rebels, once image-bearers who ruined ourselves and necessitated His righteous judgment of us. The whole of history is really the fallen history of wilderness dwellers who have been expelled from the Garden of Eden. No matter how good John was, the clue was in his God-ordained name, meaning *grace*. If John in his received goodness were to make it back to the Garden of Eden, he would depend not on *his* goodness but on that of JESUS. When placed in close proximity to the perfection of Jesus, John like us was a 6, not a 7. In Christ alone is completion, prefigured by the 7th day of creation; rest for the soul; Our rest—to be in Him.

Mary and we are to "behold" this; to commit our thoughts and reflections to the God-man. We are to be striving to *conceive* great things in our minds. Mary, Elisabeth, John and we are nothing in and of ourselves. We would be forever "barren" if God did not do something for and in us. The scene was set for the Incarnation of the Son of God.

Historical time itself would eventually be re-ordered and re-centered around His physical birth (BC-AD). Geography would soon be propelled via the mighty Roman Empire which would unwittingly serve the interests of the Gospel, each sinful Caesar unconsciously furthering Christ's interests: "Fear not: for I *am* with thee: I will bring thy seed from the east, and gather thee from the west; I will say to the north, Give up; and to the south, Keep not back: bring my sons from far, and my daughters from the ends of the earth" (Isa 43:5–6).

IMPOSSIBLE

God's will is to thwart our towers of Babel, and so He has limited us to a handful of decades of life so as to frustrate the interplanetary ambitions of our soaring egos; we must shortly meet our Maker and give account for every thought, word and deed had whilst dwelling here, according to His moral law which is written on our hearts. Even as some dream and are actively plotting the colonization of Mars so as to bring humanity into the next stage of its phoney rags to riches 'evolution' narrative, the Lord is permitting wars and diseases and catastrophes to occur so as to render these lofty plans impossible.

We may read "impossible" from different perspectives; the Gospel era perspective, for instance, in which death is not death and life (as we know it) is not life. As for Joseph, Mary, Zacharias and Elisabeth, they found to their ceaseless joy that the Savior had finally come. The types, symbols and pictures of the Old Testament had been pointing that way; to a more glorious age which we may call the New Testament, in which the Antitype had come to fulfill every type.

Another perspective might be that mankind would finally be able to overcome that time-honored division between Jew and Gentile. That apparently impenetrable wall of ethnic, racial, religious, blood-line identity would now be dissolvable; the people of God could be liberated from the linguistic, cultural, ethnic curse of the frustrated Tower of Babel, for all who love the Lord Jesus Christ find themselves living in a brotherly-sisterly way with believers from all areas of Earth.

We see how the most "impossible" thing on the face of this planet is not mountains or militaries or stupendous concrete structures, but the human heart. Who can soften it, reason with it, grant it humility, self-knowledge and gracious desire for forgiveness from its Creator and peace with its fellow beings? The human heart is the source of all the world's problems; with renewed hearts this world would be a virtual Garden of Eden. MAGA might be much in the news-cycle of the 2020s, but MEGA has been God's plan in eternity—to Make Earth Great Again by making a new heaven and earth, the original earth having been ruined by the deceitful, treacherous, sinful human heart's rebellion.

Wherever two or three formerly barren, now renewed, softened, humbled hearts are gathered in Christ's name, there alone is the possibility of true and lasting joy, peace, and love. Outside of Christ there is no true peace or true forgiveness, for "He that *hath no rule over his own spirit is like* a city *that is* broken down, *and* without walls" (Prov 25:28). As with the two Koreas of our day, men can put a fragile, reluctant armistice in place, yet only when a soul comes to live "through Christ Jesus" can there be "the peace of God, which passeth all understanding" (Phil 4:7).

WILLING HANDMAID

Another difference from Zacharias' encounter is that Mary gets the final word; her responsive, joyful, expectant heart full of zeal overflows with sound doctrine and she is granted angelic approval ordained of God. We are thus instructed in the right use of our ears and tongues. If our hearts are in tune with God's word, we may listen to the word of God with due reverence but also glean the good news of God's salvation which ought to make us overflow with praise and adoration. It is not that we sing hymns and pray because we have to, but because our hearts are overflowing—we want to. There is a world of difference between *have to* (outward religion) and *want to* (heart religion).

"Mary said" whereas Zacharias was struck dumb. Mary carried in her womb the Word incarnate whereas Zacharias' first word after his temporary rebuke was *John*, or *Grace*. Thus he communicated through the writing hand rather than the speaking mouth. We need to believe that the word of God *is* the word of God; only then will we hear it as we ought. God has inclined the human hand to write exactly what He has ordained to be written.

The status of "handmaid" is the feminine equivalent of the apostle Paul's oft used *doulos* or *bondslave*, if our modern ears can bear it; we must add "willing" to complete the phrase. While flesh desires mastery over flesh, the Spirit-filled willingly seeks and loves to be God's servant, knowing that this is to follow the example of Christ who, while Kings of kings, became Servant of servants. Anything we can do in our strength, He did better. Anything we do for Him can only be done through Him. We can only serve Him because He first came to be the Perfect Servant.

Mary's voice was uplifted to affirm God's ways over hers. As the Reformers would do centuries later, she would go to the roots (*ad fontes*), starting from the foundation of Sola Scriptura (Only Scripture) before venturing forth. She would not want to move one millimeter from God's word; she would pray that all her doings might be "according to thy word."

We who claim to be of the same ilk; Reformed, Calvinistic, Biblical . . . how truly do we hold to Sola Scriptura? Can we really bear the holy, burning light of God's Word being concentrated through the magnifying-glass of self-examination and sincere meditation? Are we really willing to put to death every pet sin, cast out every dusty idol lurking in the shadows? Do we resemble Zacharias's doubt or Mary's faith?

Then, "the angel departed from her." Angels have their place; we ours. The wonder of the Incarnation is that God would lower Himself to our level, sin excepted. Angels "desire to look into" (1 Pet 1:12) such things, to know more profoundly what it means to be redeemed from death. Such Gospel marvels are not for the angels, for they are either ever loyal, or they are "reserved in everlasting chains" (Jude 6)—forever damned.

11

A great encounter

> "And Mary arose in those days, and went into the hill country with haste, into a city of Juda; and entered into the house of Zacharias, and saluted Elisabeth. And it came to pass, that, when Elisabeth heard the salutation of Mary, the babe leaped in her womb; and Elisabeth was filled with the Holy Ghost:" (Luke 1:39-41)

WOMEN WERE AT THE forefront of the Incarnation, as they were at the Crucifixion and, for that matter, Resurrection. Mary "arose" to make the trip to Elisabeth, which could have taken days or weeks, depending on the route and mode of transport. What must the angels have thought and sang as Mary began her blessed trip.

Yet how much grander and more glorious was the trip taken from heaven to earth by our blessed Savior. He of course knew and knows all things; nevertheless, He did not flinch from what was to come. Like a warrior soon to descend into battle, "The LORD hath made bare his holy arm in the eyes of all the nations; and all the ends of the earth shall see the salvation of our God." (Isa 52:10). There simply is no way to fathom the depths to which He would descend for the love of His bride, the international, Jewish-Gentile Church. He launched Himself into the fray of turbulent humanity;

then, appearing in meekness, His hidden strength would destroy the power of sin, death and the devil.

Wise commentators have speculated over when exactly the Incarnation took place and have pondered over the phrase "with haste." Mary felt inclined to be with her cousin Elisabeth at the "sixth month"; literally true; typically, man's number. The male to be born within her would be every bit a human being; albeit a perfect Adam, a supreme Adam, sinless in every way.

She felt moved by the Holy Spirit to be in Juda; most probably Hebron, a city peculiar to the priests in which Zacharias' family would have lived. As Mary would wend her way up to a higher, more privileged priestly "hill country," the Lord Jesus would ascend from humiliation in the lowly feeding-trough and wrath of Calvary to eventually occupy the highest heavenly throne again. He would minister as High Priest on our behalf, presenting the death of Himself as the only acceptable offering, for nothing less could suffice.

Talking of Juda, we might recall that "The scepter shall not depart from Judah, nor a lawgiver from between his feet, until Shiloh come; and unto him *shall* the gathering of the people *be*. Binding his foal unto the vine, and his ass's colt unto the choice vine; he washed his garments in wine, and his clothes in the blood of grapes: His eyes *shall be* red with wine, and his teeth white with milk" (Gen 49:10–12). Our Christmas cards might focus on the physical commencement and crib-dwelling in Bethlehem but let us not forget that the King of kings first descended an infinite distance in wondrous, voluntary humiliation, down to the womb of the virgin, most probably in the place where the priests dwelled and where other notable Old Testament souls like Isaac had their being; impossible to convey in a Christmas card.

The King descended, dear soul, from heaven, for sinners such as you. He ever remained the King and yet permitted Himself to become microscopically small in the womb of Mary for His victorious plan of salvation to be activated. It began, from our human perspective, at a time in which the political and religious world was not ready. It never is.

The plan of salvation has not yet been completed; the last time I checked the news, we still dwell in a world desperately full of sin, darkness, disease, war and death. The final day has not yet come. The final elect one has not yet been released, Lazarus-like, from the death sentence of their trespasses and sins.

IN THE HOUSE

Within the Lord's eternal reign and purview, we exist because He created us. He existed forever before we were made; compared to Him we are but things of nothingness, even less than nothingness. Nevertheless, it has been the will of God first to create us and then to implicate Himself in our lives so as to accommodate Himself in a way which we can comprehend Him, insofar as He enables us.

After her long and tiring, self-sacrificial, God-centered, Christ-exalting, Spirit-filled journey to her cousin Elisabeth, Mary "entered into the house." Just as Mary entered the house, God the Son entered the human race at a unique moment we call the Incarnation, maybe too glibly and thoughtlessly, for it was the most remarkable thing ever to have had happened up until that point. The original creation of earth and heaven had been, up until then, the most remarkable thing, but the Incarnation far surpassed it, for the Creator compressed Himself into microscopic format to be born as a man; to come into fruition as a mortal being yet still fully being God!

"House" is another term too often used without reflection, for what is this world if not a house containing God's house, the church. To be in that house is the goal of existence. Not to be in that house is the worst thing imaginable, for it means to face the prospect of judgment followed by everlasting punishment. To be in God's house is the grand and only quest of human beings. Only through Christ may we have a sure hope of entering God the Father's "house" which we are told has "many mansions" (John 14:2).

A house can be a blessed or a terrible thing, depending on whose it is. King Hezekiah was told to get his house in order because he was facing death. Our houses should be places of preparation for eternity rather than fortresses of worldly indulgence; warmth and godly zeal rather than refuges from serious contemplation, mere electronic playpens. I ask myself whether my own house is in order. If my life were to end today, am I ready? Is my house prepared?

The head of the house, Zacharias, is mentioned first, for human, earthly marriage is a picture of Christ the Bridegroom with Church the Bride. Zacharias was a godly man whom God remembered and who remembered God. Yet Elisabeth it was whom Mary "saluted," for she was the carrier of the best of humanity, John, full of grace. The word "saluted" could equally be *embraced*, *kissed* and *hugged*. This was a homecoming of sorts, for these two believers were granted special blessings, as every gathering of believers is when meeting in fellowship and communion, even two or three.

How many people do we salute in a day, and yet how many of them do we recognize as those with whom we share an eternal, everlasting bond, stronger than blood? Perhaps saluting is better than embracing because Christ came to this earth in great condescension, love and pity for this sin-soaked, benighted world. The bride is not yet ready to be fully embraced; the marriage is not yet fully consummated for the world still rolls on and is too often stained with tears, disappointments and frustrations, God's people included. There will come that last day when the Bride will leave *her* house, this earth, for good and be received into her Bridegroom's Father's eternally glorious house forever.

THE BABE LEAPED

God comes to man, not the other way around. When placed in a paradise of free will and deathless abundance, we squandered it by rebelling against our Creator. The subsequent history of mankind has been of God visiting man in covenant-keeping mercy, whilst the mixed-multitude of Old Testament Israel largely rebelled, ran away, mingled idolatry with true, heart religion, believing God would allow it.

Currently in the West, progressive values so-called, including the right to abort one's baby, change one's gender, get married to one's own gender and put a depressed or frail person to death are echoes of the Tower of Babel in that we are trying to achieve heaven our way, replacing God's will and glory with our will and our glory. We don't just want to rival God; we want to be in the place of God. Who but flawed image bearers of God would have the audacity to attempt it!

God's response is and ever has been to continue visiting souls one by one, in ways and means of His own choosing. Thus, Elisabeth "heard" God speaking to her through His servant Mary, as we hear God speaking to us through His ministers. We do not seek God; He seeks us. We like Mary find ourselves in the hill country of our lives, with the various ups and downs of God's Fatherly providence towards us, to which we have no right outside of His grace.

God seeks us, enters our midst and speaks to us in holy "salutation," for the Bible is a personal book which reads and touches persons in their inmost core. If God hadn't sought us we would never have sought Him. If He hadn't called to us through the proclamation of His word, we would never have responded to it. We are the visited not the visitor, for the Gospel message is always a response to God's call. It is of the LORD, not man, as Jonah learned in that most deep and watery place.

Then, "the babe leaped in her womb," as our hearts leap within us when we consider Christ who has entered our lives through no merit of our own. Grace-filled John is the prototypical recipient of unmerited favor, unwarranted blessing. When the *God-man* meets the *best man* the best man is convicted of his own unworthiness and leaps for joy at the prospect of the God-man covering his every sin; past, present and future. The *best man* is content with being nothing so that the *God-man* might be everything. "He must increase, but I *must* decrease" (John 3:30) would be his motto text, overjoyed to be "the friend of the bridegroom" (John 3:29).

God the "Holy Ghost" then "filled" Elisabeth yet, as Elisabeth's name implies, we do not depend on feelings or movements of the Holy Ghost within but rather rest the whole weight of our salvation upon the oath of God's word. Our hearts may deceive us "but the word of our God shall stand for ever" (Isa 40:8). It is possible that much of Isaiah 40–64 would have been the substance of many future sermons by John, "the voice" of Isaiah 40:3, which we know alludes to him as he rightfully claimed: "I *am* the voice" (John 1:23).

GETTING IT RIGHT

> "And she spake out with a loud voice, and said, Blessed *art* thou among women, and blessed *is* the fruit of thy womb. And whence *is* this to me, that the mother of my Lord should come to me? For, lo, as soon as the voice of thy salutation sounded in mine ears, the babe leaped in my womb for joy. And blessed *is* she that believed: for there shall be a performance of those things which were told her from the Lord." (Luke 1:42–45)

From the overflow of feelings come words. We do not merely utter praise to God out of cold duty but confess the name of God warmly, treasuring it in our hearts, unable to restrain words which come forth like precious nectar. We may have sung hymns as a child, perhaps at school, but only when born again sing them from the heart with a "loud voice." It is not the desire to be heard but for the truth to ring out like a bell; from, to and for God whom we adore.

We must be so careful to avoid those pitfalls of Marian worship which have plagued the church over many centuries, or for that matter, sink into mere formalism or human-centered worship which is not Godward. Mary is "blessed," yes, for she had treasure within. It is foolish to value the earthen vessel above the eternal treasure therein, whether with Mary, Spurgeon, Luther or Augustine, or whomever—we must never elevate the creature above the Creator. There is even the plague of eco-centered worship in our day, which is just as bad. Some so-called Christians elevate the temporal wellbeing of this material Earth over the eternal good of souls, to their shame.

I recall once speaking to a godly, visiting evangelist who gave a stirring lesson on the grace of God, expounding Ephesians 2:8-9 in particular. At the end, I approached him to thank him for this uplifting and instructive lesson. He looked pained and pointed up, directing praise away from self and towards God. If we are indeed blessed for Christ's sake, let us not be those who receive praise for our sake. Elisabeth showed that it is "the fruit" which she was praising, not the woman or the "womb." Likewise, when in Paul's early days as a professing believer in Christ, it was not Paul who was "glorified" but "God in me" (Gal 1:24).

Equally, we would not be those who withhold audible praise, thinking that our silence somehow speaks a thousand words. We would not retreat into monkish caves and mystic cells to escape the world; although appearing holy, this is not the narrow way of bearing Christ's yoke but the easy way of obsessing over self.

OVERWHELMED YET OVERJOYED

Mary was, in one sense, "the mother of my Lord" but in a deeper, more biblically balanced sense, carried within her the Lord of her, she being a mother chosen for a unique, ordained purpose. The Lord chose to inhabit a womb for nine months; nevertheless, He in no sense was less than Lord throughout His whole time in womb and on earth.

Through the mystery of conception and gestation, labor and birth, the Creator chose to become incarnate and dwell among the creatures He had made in His image. Similarly, the Lord appears among us today, dwelling amidst very ordinary, unworthy sinners like us. It has not been His wont to dwell among the rich, great and powerful of this sin-sick world although at times He has; on the whole, His glory is more often present among the unimpressive, feeble and ordinary ones of earth: "But God hath chosen the foolish things of the world to confound the wise; and God hath chosen the weak things of the world to confound the things which are mighty" (1 Cor 1:27).

Elisabeth is perplexed and overwhelmed by this happening "to me," despite having set out in life to be spiritually minded and blessed. She, like her husband, was a humble believer who was going about her daily devotions and duties and had no thought of such an honor being bestowed on her. Until the day when Zacharias was so shaken and stirred by angelic encounter, she was the supportive wife, he the faithful fulfiller of religious affairs and functions, in no sense anticipating or expecting what was to come.

Until the day when Joseph was amazed by angelic communication, he was going about his daily duties, unassuming and humble. We do not know why "me" and not another; whatever we have been prepared for, it is of the Lord. Maybe the beginnings of a great awakening or revival might happen through you and some fellow believers who feel moved to meet for prayer in a strange and more earnest than usual way. If we knew what was to come ahead of time, we might be tempted to become puffed up or might recoil with ungodly fear.

Women are noticeable in the New Testament age, complementing the more male-dominated Old Testament age of patriarchs and prophets. The dignity, special operation and deep mystery of pregnancy is elevated and woman ennobled to greater heights than before. Mary could have gone to Zacharias, but the Lord drew her to Elisabeth. As aforementioned, women were prominent at the Cross and at the Tomb. Men were slower to act in humble faith and simple love for the Lord.

Through the womb comes life, and through these two women's wombs came the best man of earth and the God-man from heaven; earth's best man then heaven's Bridegroom. None of us may be better than John, yet John was nothing before the Lord Jesus. He was a man taken up with reverent love for Christ. He believed that the key to Christianity is Christ. The key to the Bible is Christ. The key to God's kingdom and eternal life is Christ. The key to Judgment Day—Christ.

HAVE YOU HEARD?

A baby's sense of hearing is well developed, the inner ear being perfectly formed in the womb. Although normal for a baby to leap in the womb from the simple joy of being alive, here something else was occurring—"Deep calleth unto deep" (Ps 42:7), for this "babe" was enlivened by the Holy Spirit even before delivery from the womb, as we are told in verse 15.

In verse 44 we are told of the "joy" which unborn-yet-born-again John had. Although such a solemn and holy thing, joy for the born-again convert is present and will be present throughout our earthly pilgrimages, not constantly but consistently; a blessed foretaste of the glory to come.

Instrumentality seems to be here, for God uses Mary as an instrument through whom to speak to Elisabeth and John. Similarly, none of us claims to have seen or spoken with God but, when faithfully preached, we experienced His word impressing itself upon our hearts, convicting and uplifting us as we heard of the terrifying exactitude and holiness of the Law, then the relieving Gospel "salutation" which, in God's perfect time, caused us to have "leaped" inwardly.

In a sense, the blessed preacher of God's word comes bearing Christ within the womb of his sermon, while the receptive listener to God's word in accord with God's will becomes alive in a most real, inward way. We are dealing with things which are hidden and unseen to the eye; the eye so easily led astray and tempted by the vanity-fair of this alluring world. The ear is a more reliable conduit through which the Lord has chosen to save souls, for faith comes by hearing.

And how is it that a soul comes to life and is born-again? Such a thing is a profound mystery. The soul understands things in a way which the mind and heart must serve, not master; we are souls which have bodies, not the other way round. One soul may attend a church or chapel and hear 1,000 sermons, none of which leads to salvation. Another may hear just one sermon or a fragment of a Gospel message, even online, and be saved in an instant. It depends on the Lord who determines all things in His immutable and perfect will.

MARY BELIEVED

Mary "believed" and it was credited to her as righteousness, as with Abraham: "For what saith the scripture? Abraham believed God, and it was counted unto him for righteousness" (Rom 4:3). It was not anything good in Mary which was praised and rewarded, so much as her receptivity to God's word; for she received it "as it is in truth, the word of God, which effectually" worked in her (1 Thess 2:13). There is all the difference in the world between belief and unbelief; we must remember that it is the Lord who graciously opens hearts and elucidates minds, not anything of human persuasion or coercion. All we can do is ask; He alone bestows.

From her childhood lessons of instruction and hearing rabbinical preaching, Mary would have had much of God's word within her. She would have known many of the psalms by heart and been steeped in a tradition of great reverence and respect for the Scriptures. Mary's experience of angelic visitation was extraordinary; nevertheless, it was in keeping with the Scriptures, in particular Genesis 3:15, ergo she believed that God would do what He said, for God's will could and would not be thwarted by man's will. Mary simply "believed" that what God had said to Eve was finally to be completed in herself, through the fruit of her womb.

We find an echo of "from the Lord" in Eve's similar "from the LORD" of Genesis 4:1. We ought not minimize or under-emphasize the fact that every godly woman since the time of Eve, up to the time of Christ, would have at times been prayerfully wondering whether the promised Seed might take up residence within her.

There was no false humility in Mary, no attempt to deny Elisabeth's thanksgiving and praise at what the Lord was doing in her life. Mary's subsequent psalm would reveal the extent to which she was a woman who knew the Scriptures, desiring God's glory and the release of millions of captives from the prison-house of sin. Mary needed salvation as much as the next woman, so she looked to that ultimate "performance" or fulfilment which would lead from womb to tomb to eternity.

There is great joy in being used instrumentally by God, His plan being fulfilled in and through you. God's ends, His goal, His plan—unalterable; even so, we are not always the content conduits we should be. Discontentment can creep in and become ours if we are not careful, else Paul's exhortation to seek "godliness with contentment" (1 Tim 6:6) would be superfluous.

The happiest Christian is one who is joyfully given to the will of God being done in his or her life; not in a passive or fatalistic but victorious, anticipatory way, trembling at the prospect of the glory to come. Mary's unique role was atypical and extra-ordinary; yet her faith and humility were normative and regulatory for all believers. To follow her in this secondary way would be a great blessing for us. Never is she to be worshipped, however, in any way, shape or form, for the First Commandment reads: "Thou shalt have no other gods before me." (Exod 20:3).

12

A psalm out of time

> "And Mary said, My soul doth magnify the Lord, and my spirit hath rejoiced in God my Savior." (Luke 1:46–47)

MARY'S NEW TESTAMENT TEN verse Magnificat, so-called, is equivalent to Hannah's Song of Thanksgiving in the Old Testament; in fact, greater because it more clearly reveals the project, plan and mission of the Second Person of the Godhead, whereas Hannah's song rejoices more generally in the Godhead.

Hannah's heart passively, meditatively rejoices in the Lord whereas Mary's soul more actively desires to "magnify" the Lord. Both prayers read more like psalms rather than spontaneous prayers, due no doubt to both believers' knowledge of the Scriptures, large portions of which they would have known by heart. Mary and Joseph would have heard the psalms of David read continually at their local temple. The psalm framework would be in their bones.

The humility of Mary's "My" was based on a personal assurance that she was the Lord's. Not all Jews could say the same, just as the majority which identifies as 'Christian' does not actually know anything of the second birth. Hannah and Mary were both submissive when it came to letting the fruit of their wombs, their firstborns, go. The "My" of rejoicing and magnifying was spiritual, their "affection" set "on things above, not on things on the earth" (Col 3:2).

Bodily health is of course important for we are charged with being good stewards thereof. But one's "soul" is of far greater importance; God is primarily concerned with it. The modern field known as Psychology, from the word *psyche*, has appropriated the language of the soul, seeking to explain it through materialism, or natural "science falsely so called" (1 Tim 6:20). The Bible is a spiritually focused book, using spiritual language which only a spiritually minded person can discern. Until one receives spiritual life in the soul, the life-changing truth of the Bible remains locked.

Paradoxically, the life that is most spiritual is most at peace in the body, while the life that is devoid of spiritual life progressively forfeits any chance of peace in a body which is doomed to death and judgment. *"There is* no peace, saith my God, to the wicked," the prophet tells us (Isa 57:21). This means no spiritual peace, for there is only spiritual peace; all that is not spiritual peace is temporal and finite peace which is not peace.

The concept of "magnify" is perhaps even clearer now than it was in the times before the magnifying glass was invented (circa AD 1250 by Roger Bacon). Everyone who wears spectacles is in fact a walking visual aid, for the notion of such technology is that the glass has been engineered so as to restore perfect sight to the wearer, just as the person who is miraculously 'born again' only then begins to see life properly, for the first time. That person realizes that their former, pre-conversion life was actually death.

The magnification of faith claims no glory and draws no attention to itself; its job is to become virtually invisible in its service to the things which are to meet the mind. Glasses are but the means of vision, just as faith is but the gracious means of spiritual understanding, " . . . and that not of yourselves . . . " (Eph 2:8).

God therefore teaches us through Mary that the believer's highest calling is to become so full of Christ that people almost overlook you as their focus is on Christ. The preachers who have been most valued and appreciated have been those whose sermons have been full of the Scriptures, so as to magnify Christ; pulpit servants rather than platform performers.

The Christians who have been mighty magnifiers in the hand of God; the apostle Paul, Augustine, Luther or moderns like Spurgeon, Ryle, Pink, Lloyd-Jones, Mahan, Masters, Thackway to name but a few, have sought to reduce themselves within their sermons so that their hearers' minds may be filled with "the fulness of him that filleth all in all" (Eph 1:23). If a preacher becomes too present and full of himself within his sermon, Christ is not there.

As the Lord worked mysteriously upon that vast mass of fluid, watery matter at the dawn of time, the Lord would work even more profoundly upon the womb of this chosen woman, to bring to birth the only righteous life that ever would walk upon this earth. His righteous life must be imputed to us to render us 'just'; His risen life must be imparted to us to keep us sanctified.

Importantly, it is not her womb which Mary talks of, but her soul. It is the full weight and essence of who Mary is which is being invoked here rather than some vainglorious, self-seeking, bodily adulation. She would be appalled by what she has become, if she could see it. The visual beatification of a perpetually virginal mediatrix in heaven is abomination in the sight of God.

MARY WORSHIPS

Verses 46-47 seem to encompass and anticipate; they encompass the spirit of Hannah's Old Testament thanksgiving for the Lord's provision of a child; they anticipate the life-giving Cross-work of Christ who would first be born, then live a wholly righteous life in the flesh, then permit this life to be offered up as an atonement for us, then ascend back up to glory to reign on High where He is today.

Mary's emphasis, moved by the Holy Spirit, is on "spirit" rather than flesh. Aside from her miraculous conception, her gestation, labor and birth would be the same as every other woman's, mingled with physical pain, strains, stretches, broken waters and final delivery. No woman exists in the state of Genesis 2 (or man, for that matter); the joy and hope which birth brings is accompanied by that which reminds us of the Fall.

Theologians have argued that soul (psyche) and spirit (pneuma) are interchangeable, or the same thing but looked at in different ways. In the context of these verses, soul would seem to be the whole weight of a person, responsible and accountable to God; spirit would seem to indicate the part of us which more purely concerns itself with the things of heaven. God, after all, is referred to as "a Spirit" (John 4:24) and Jesus is referred to as having given up the spirit (ghost) in the 4 synoptic accounts of His death, whereas the soul of Jesus is associated more with the weight and burden of living on earth: "Deliver my soul from the sword; my darling from the power of the dog" (Ps 22:20).

Mary, therefore, concerned with the things of the Spirit, uses the latter term here. Her whole life (soul) may seek to be a magnifying glass for God's glory, whereas her spiritual faculty (spirit) actively explores that which will bring her into heavenly communion with her Creator.

Mary worships God as we should. She does not make an idol out of One Person within the Godhead; some seem only to worship the Spirit, especially in 'charismatic' circles, while others almost forget the deity of the Son in their efforts to exalt the Father, such as in modern Anglicanism or Catholicism. It was the whole Godhead which was involved in the salvation mission on earth. In everything Jesus did, the Godhead was involved. Even that divine turning away from Jesus on the Cross was a part of the divine plan, as we read in John 17:4.

The original text reads *God the Savior of me* rather than 'God my Savior' and this is perhaps helpful in elucidating the point. God can at no point be divided or compartmentalized; God works within Himself in complete harmony and Oneness, and in plurality. God the Father sent God the Son; God the Son willingly came; God the Spirit seals the sinner with a new nature, thus the Triune Godhead effectually effectuates salvation. Salvation is personal because it is the salvation of individual persons, ergo God is "my

Savior." Equally, salvation was initiated in eternity by God, accomplished in time by God, and has eternal ramifications.

Many in our day claim to be spiritual but not religious; to love Jesus but not God or love the church but not the congregants or love the Bible but not its application. God works in Mary's words here to guard against these false distinctions. Just as Jesus was, is and ever will be 100% Divine, equal to the Father, so the Bible is the only source of authority on earth by which we may devise statements of faith and construct systematic theologies.

Thankfully, like those noble Bereans, we can be those who have "received the word with all readiness of mind, and searched the scriptures daily, whether those things were so" (Acts 17:11). We should not invest any human preacher with that same degree of absolute authority. While we have been granted many true expositors of God's word over the centuries, the moment we find ourselves turning to any one of them ahead of God's word, as somehow being on a par with it, let us rebuke ourselves: "God forbid: yea, let God be true, but every man a liar . . . " (Rom 3:4).

HER UNIQUE CALLING

> "For he hath regarded the low estate of his handmaiden: for, behold, from henceforth all generations shall call me blessed. For he that is mighty hath done to me great things; and holy *is* his name. And his mercy *is* on them that fear him from generation to generation." (Luke 1:48–50)

It is important to note that it is not Mary *per se* whom the Lord regards with respect; rather, Mary in her "low estate". The lower one is in one's eyes, the truer one is in God's, for we are not in the condition in which we were first were at Creation; we are in a fallen condition, "shapen in iniquity; and in sin" conceived (Ps 51:5). The less we think of ourselves the truer we are, the readier for God's grace. Our fallen condition deludes us into to believing we're good enough as we are by nature.

God our heavenly Father regards us in our sin, lowness, misery and ruin, and has respect for our acknowledging and confessing this. If we yield our lives to become His *doulas* or *handmaiden*, perhaps best translated for our modern ear as *willing servant*, He will greatly bless and use us. It is hard to imagine a message which is more inimical and repulsive to the worldly modern mind; the very idea of humility, submission, servitude and sinfulness flies in the face of all we strive to project about ourselves in our day. These words have lost the currency they once had.

Who looks in the mirror and sees a sinner? Who in our day aspires to be a spiritual butler, footman, nanny or servant? Who cares for the things of the soul over the things of the body; things of God rather than of man? Sobering questions demand a considered response. To become more than we are we need to be less than we are, for our root problem is that we do not truly know who what we are—in God's purview repulsive and wormly, corrupt to the core and cursed compared with what we were on Day Six.

Mary does not hide this but holds it in holy meditation. She does not deny she is a lowly *doulas*, worthy of nothing but condemnation. She does not seek a false humility, overdramatizing her "low estate", calling it hopeless or irremediable. She starts with God, "He" and ends with God, "Him" in the original, locating herself within His pitying regard of her. She feels herself to be an object of His mercy and therefore rejoices. It is not blind faith because based on the Scriptures; not blind joy because based on spiritual experience.

She also apprehends something of her unique calling—to be a bearer of the blessed child, the Holy One, the Seed, the God-man through whom the elect would be redeemed. Her soul, like a magnifying-glass, a ready receptacle through which the Lord would shine; her spirit content to dwell in His presence, rejoicing that God has saved her eternally; given eyes to see, spiritual discernment to know the promise of Genesis 3:15 realized in her womb.

Her eyes were on future "generations", on a radical testament covenanted in eternity, fulfilled in time. She was an active participant in the grace of God rather than a passive bystander, a good example for members of evangelical churches throughout the centuries. Once one becomes a Christian, one's life of delusion is "dead, and" one's true "life is hid with Christ in God" (Col 3:3).

One's firm desire is for others to be saved, so like Mary we look for blessing to come upon a vast multitude in future generations. She was not clinging to this world but rejoicing in the next, knowing that the new or permanent heaven and earth would be far better than this old or temporary iteration, due to the Seed which would raise up millions to populate it.

Like Saul-converted-Paul, she was a person of the world with heavenly yearnings, vaguely perceiving the triumphant Crosswork of the Seed which would lead her in later years to be ever more willing to be in heaven than on earth, "in a strait betwixt two, having a desire to depart, and to be with Christ; which is far better" (Phil 1:23).

GREAT THINGS

The dynamic power of God is beyond comprehension; it evades our ability to give it expression. We are objects of His creation; we look up at the night sky or ponder oceanic, magmatic depths and are staggered and amazed by the vastness of it. He sustains and breathes life into all, keeping it all the time, for "he is before all things, and by him all things consist" (Col 1:17). He maintains the heaven and hell which He created, solemnly declaring that such things should be.

All we see around us is winding down and diminishing in strength and longevity. But not the Lord. He has an endless abundance of everlasting power, never depleted or in need of rejuvenation. He is both Self-existent and Self-sustaining, requiring no external power source. He is the source of all power. Furthermore, our worship of Christ is right and proper for there is nothing lacking in Christ, "for it pleased *the Father* that in him should all fulness dwell" (Col 1:19). He is as much God as is the Father and is the Holy Spirit.

Mary is humbled and awed by what the Lord "hath done" to her personally. She, of all people. Why her? Simply because the Lord had created her for this purpose. She had been predestined for "great things"; the Lord Himself would deign to inhabit her womb. God the Spirit would be intimately involved with her so that she might be used to bear the Son of God who would be the Son of man in the fullest sense. He would inherit humanity but without any of its defilements.

The "great things" in store for Mary would be a blessing for the whole world, not just this Middle Eastern section thereof. If, at the dawn of time, the Lord was pleased to call His original creation *good* or *very good*, at the time of Incarnation He would call it *great* and *holy*. First Adam at creation was good. Last Adam at Incarnation was great. First Adam at creation had within him the possibility of rebellion and sin. Last Adam at Incarnation was wholly obedient; the possibility of rebellion and sin were not in him.

Sadly, believers are at times tempted at tripped up by the devil and his demons. Joyfully, believers, even at their worst, may hope in their Redeemer, remembering that His perfect life was substituted for their flawed life, pre and post conversion. Whereas with us there may be an ongoing sense of wrestling, pruning, trials, tests and growth, with Him, the devil or "prince of this world" was comprehensively thwarted, for when he encountered the righteous daily living of this Jesus of Nazareth, there was no angle for the tempter and accuser of souls to exploit, "for the prince of this world cometh, and hath nothing in me" (John 14:30).

"Holy" or Hagios is difficult for us to translate, in that we do not have a place for it in worldly society, whether ancient or modern. An *awful thing* is one translation, yet even here our sense of *awe* in *aweful* does not mean much in our day and age. We are a thoroughly awe-less generation; the only things we have eyes for are the things of human ingenuity or nature.

But we should beware of entering the presence of God; we are to seek cleansing, repentance and faith, just as every called-out believer has done through the generations. Peter was truer than most of us most of the time, when his reaction was to recoil from

Christ's holiness: "Depart from me; for I am a sinful man, O Lord." (Luke 5:8). He was confessing that, in and of himself, he did not belong with God. This is the definition of humility; a frank admission rather than a ceremonial ritual. We may crawl into a desert cave, forsaking every creature comfort, only to find pride inflating us even more than before!

God is utterly separate from us, infinitely above us, more profound than the most gifted genius or blessed prophet can start to consider. We are forbidden from entering His presence, other than through His ordained way. Who was Peter to enter Jesus' presence? Who was Mary to have "great things" done "to" her? Who are you to be granted spiritual life? Who am I to be writing about this? These are unanswerable questions—by faith we find an answer to them in the name of Christ, who is one with God, who is "holy."

The very next verse confirms this through the word "fear." We struggle with words like awe, holy and "fear" in this sense, but may rest assured in God's plans for this human rat race, His plans being more wonderful and far better than the best of ours.

BELIEVERS FEAR

We may sometimes be near despair when we consider the younger generation; those in whose hearts foolishness is bound, who know nothing and consider no one but themselves. Yet the Lord even in our day is able and willing to raise up saints from the soil of sin; such were we until we found "his mercy". We were making plans and adopting strategies to make ourselves right in our own sight, according to our thoughts.

God, however, had other things in store and was willing to give us far more than we thought to ask for. He was willing to grant us a feast of full forgiveness when we were seeking to wean ourselves from the rotting buffet of this wilderness-world, seeking to merit salvation through a contrived famine of the usual things which delight men and women. The spiritual life that we have when our eyes and ears are divinely opened is more abundant than anything we could have envisaged with our burdensome religions, be they spiritualistic or humanistic.

Mary shows us that it is not wrong for us to start with what the Lord has done in and for us personally, but we are then to go on and consider the church universal, in space and time, for "on them" the mercy of God must come and so we should be seeking the good of souls everywhere, all the time. There is no privileged corner of the planet; all must come to Christ who reigns from heaven.

If the world were to end today, there would only be two sorts of humans—those who have God's mercy and those who have it not; those who have that divine fire-blanket covering them from even the smallest hint of fiery wrath and indignation; and those who remain uncovered and exposed to the righteous judgment of God who will cast them into perdition; a state of permanent removal from the general blessings and providence of God enjoyed throughout this first creation.

The shocking thing is not that Jesus "shall set the sheep on his right hand, but the goats on the left" (Matt 25:33). The shocking thing is that those who thought they were "sheep" were in fact "goats", for they had no real relationship with God and so no real love for human souls. They may have thought they were doing good to fellow beings, but they had no love for their souls: "And these shall go away into everlasting punishment: but the righteous into life eternal" (Matt 25:46). Verses 34-45 of Matthew 25 must be interpreted spiritually; not that the body is of no regard, but that the outreach and assistance offered and granted to others must include both body and soul if it is to be of Christ.

Believers "fear" God as obedient children fear a lovingly firm parent. There is a sense of wanting parental love and approval; another of not wanting rebuke and chastisement. In fact, the worst and most fearful punishment for a child is the silence that comes with being ignored. Speaking spiritually, this is hell—to be away from the presence of our Father.

And who is it that we "fear" but "him", not another. We all too often fear man who is powerless over the soul, when we should fear God who is all powerful. We all too often worry and fret about what others think when there is only One concerning whom our fears and desires should be. The Pastor should be feared insofar as he proclaims the word of God; however, in and of himself he is but a man, often a gentle and unassuming one when not proclaiming from the pulpit.

Christ has demarcated the whole of history, "from generation" BC "to generation" AD. Who other than Mary could have known that this would be the case, especially when she was tending to her baby in the feeding-trough of a nondescript inn. Who could ever have believed or foreseen such an unlikely, humbling thing. The Seed concept remained in the minds of Jews throughout the centuries; the practical arrangements of the Seed's Incarnation were revealed only to a few foreign Magi and some unimpressive Jewish shepherds.

HE ALONE

> "He hath shewed strength with his arm; he hath scattered the proud in the imagination of their hearts. He hath put down the mighty from *their* seats, and exalted them of low degree. He hath filled the hungry with good things; and the rich he hath sent empty away. He hath holpen his servant Israel, in remembrance of *his* mercy; as he spake to our fathers, to Abraham, and to his seed for ever." (Luke 1:51–55)

From the dawn of time, proud man and proud angel have been "scattered" from their original positions. Adam and Eve were banished from the Garden of Eden, Lucifer and possibly a third of the angels from heaven.

We tend to over-estimate our abilities and crave a worldly light rather than pray for the true Light to shine through us. We have schemed and connived to be the captains of our souls rather than be moved by the breeze of the Holy Spirit; faithful vessels in our Savior's hand.

From God's view, He "beheld, and *there was* no man; even among them, and *there was* no counsellor, that, when I asked of them, could answer a word. Behold, they *are* all vanity; their works *are* nothing; their molten images *are* wind and confusion." (Isa 41:28-29). We are thus directed instead to "Behold my servant" (Isa 42:1). God's servant was the One and only who would live a righteous life; in Adam, no one else would or could.

Christ alone has lived that prophesied, righteous and godly life in the flesh. Our righteousness and godliness are through Him. God's "strength" is not one of mere destruction, as Satan's, but of perfecting and completing what He started when He first made man. He has the strength to re-work self-righteous, recalcitrant clay such as we are, so that we progressively become godly vessels of grace. It is far easier to smash, destroy, obliterate than to bear with, incline and re-mold. It may be that "with his arm" God casts aside our vain pretensions and pride; but with his hand that He fashions us anew.

More impressive still is the fact that the "imagination of" our "hearts" does not give us a moment's respite; our old nature remains as if to show us what we would have been if we had been left untouched by God. It also warns us not to turn from our Maker, for by His holy dynamism we are sustained and upheld. The bubbling cauldron of our hearts has an endless supply of alternative plans and prospects ready to well up within if given the chance. Yet if the heart is right with God, the cauldron cools and our old nature loses much of its power.

THE LAST ADAM

In a sense, our race was initially exalted under King Adam; he was granted dominion over the planet, charged with the royal duty of subduing and tending it. Yet he was tragically and rapidly humbled, so we awaited the last Adam, He who did things the other way round—from a place of infinite glory stooping down to our level, humbling Himself on our behalf before being raised back up to glory with the addition of a human body, thence to reign over those who were created to bear His name.

If the first Adam was raised up from the dust but became proud and fell, the last Adam descended from eternal glory to the dust, permitting Himself to be falsely accused, unjustly condemned, then returned again to His glory. Strictly speaking, "no man" did anything to Christ which wasn't foreknown and fore planned—after laying down his human "life" He "took" it up again (John 10:17–18); thus, He was not merely the passive victim but active agent within His own victorious mission.

The original sense of "put down" is even stronger, suggesting overweening pride, stubbornness and rebellion. We need not only be gently "put down" but pulled off our pedestals which seek to emulate the glory of God and replace it with a version more pleasing to us. There are not just idols without but idols within; we would, if we could, accept the worship of ourselves from others, becoming princes, potentates, popes according to our own desire. In our crafty deceitfulness, we would justify and rationalize such power-grabs, masking them with a veneer of godly instrumentality.

The first dawning of repentance shows us what we are in God's sight: "wretched, and miserable, and poor, and blind, and naked" (Rev 3:17), incurably diseased and ripe for judgment. Rather than the "mighty" dynasties we would build if left to our own devices, what we really need is spiritual in-sight to see and continually be reminded of our true nature revealed in God's word: "Remember therefore how thou hast received and heard, and hold fast, and repent ... " (Rev 3:3).

Once we have been granted such a sight of self as to be repulsed by it, we will feel compelled to abandon those manifold "seats" of self-empowerment the world would place before us. That is not to say we cannot fulfill certain roles in certain organizations for God's glory, but more to emphasize first and foremost our servanthood of King Jesus—we are either His beloved subjects or incorrigible rebels fit for destruction.

God's ways are not ours; when we would seek to be "exalted" in our own eyes, God may humble us to the dust so that we may begin to live in His reality rather man's delusion. The best man, John the Baptist, a mere babe at this point, would later express his utter unworthiness to even presume to tie the shoe-laces of the God-man (John 1:27). What about us?

We ought not try to descend one "degree" lower than His incarnation and crucifixion or seek to exalt ourselves one "degree" higher than His resurrection and ascension. The wisest and best thing for us to do is to rest in Jesus, "complete in Him" (Col 2:10).

IN CHRIST

The sweet Psalmist of Israel tells us that his "cup runneth over" (Ps 23:5). Likewise, our Lord in His authoritative preface to Christian living (the Beatitudes), explains that those terms hunger and thirst need to be spiritualized. We had no clue, in other words, until we are saved, that our souls were "empty"; that there was no spiritual food or water to nourish and sustain them. We only thought of our stomachs. We didn't think we needed to be "filled" with anything until the day the Lord showed us something of the reality of our selves.

From that day forth, we have understood more of what Psalm 23 and Matthew 5 are about; we have been given to understand that, if the Lord had not "filled" us with spiritually "good things," we would continue to be ticking time bombs, waiting to explode into judgment then hell. Moreover, we now rejoice in being filled to overflowing. We have no fear that the capacity and resources of our Lord will run out; they never will. And if any more capacity for or containing of grace is required from us the creature, He will provide.

Along with John the Baptist, we have been asked to do things *for* our Lord Jesus; this is His will. However, the reality is that a cup can do nothing to honor an ocean except it be "filled", again and again. If we could do all things that ever could be done, it would still be but a drop in the ocean of His eternal goodness. And let us not envy other cups, for we each have exactly what has been ordained. It is foolish to wish to be another cup or to have what another has, for it is filled with the same ocean of divine love. We are one in the ocean of Christ.

Interestingly, these categories of "the hungry" and "the rich" are grammatically in the active present participle; not merely "hungry" but hungering every day, hopefully for spiritual things; not merely "rich" but always growing richer in worldly things of no value to the soul; hopefully not so with us! In Christ, there is no more ongoing restlessness and desperate endeavor, no more craving for worldly treasure. The day we knew the Lord Jesus was the day we died to all that; the day we died was the day we started to live no longer in ourselves but in Him. What a relief.

To desire to be among "the rich" in the wrong sense is to desire to be self-sufficient, that is, filled with our own riches on this desert-island earth. If we get the balance wrong, we might be aligning ourselves with those whose choice has been to reject the evidence of creation, the cry of conscience, the historical, global out-reach of churches which faithfully minister God's holy word. They are to be "sent away" to a place which is even more "empty," wherein dwells no good thing. The riches they have now will perish, but so too will they go on to become forever being impoverished, forever hating God.

If you fear this, dear soul, then do something about it while there is time. Will you be hungering for treasure or hankering for trash?

GOD KNEW US

A whole nation may be compared to a *child* which is an equally acceptable translation of the original word which can also mean *servant* as in "servant Israel." Anyone who has experienced the love of a parent for a child knows something of the jealous, protective love that is stronger than marauding invaders or wild animals. Is there anything a parent wouldn't do for their child? Is there anything fiercer than a parent whose emotions are stirred and powers heightened because their child's life is in danger?

"Holpen" also carries the notion of *partaking* in the experiences of the one being helped. A parent will feel the pain of a child, almost as if that experience were being inflicted upon *them*. What formidable and unfathomable love God has for all for whom He would descend and be put to death in substitution, rather than allow them to perish and be cast away. He would not merely save from afar but would dwell among; come to meet us where we are.

The involvement of God in the affairs of His children is what sets true religion apart from false. Formalistic, ritualistic, mythical religions have a distant, estranged view of their god or gods. True religion portrays God as He is; a loving Heavenly Father, a deeply concerned, willingly obedient Heavenly Son, a pitying, powerful Holy Spirit. The Godhead has dealt with millions of sinners personally; each adopted child is not only a unique creation but is uniquely loved for who they are in Christ.

Jacob would not just pray to God but would be a wrestler with God; God the Son would appear to Him and allow Jacob personally to relate to Him, to be known more intimately in his mind, his heart, to physically grapple with Him in a theophany which is hard for us to comprehend. Jacob would soon thereafter be known as Israel and so that filial, adopted connection is the way we are to be; both children who have been adopted by God our Father, and those who become strengthened by grace through faith so that we learn not only to live by faith but to walk by it, as we go along.

Israel would be uniquely privileged and blessed, but child Israel would not be perfected while on earth or exist trouble-free. True Israel—all those adopted by God—would be prevented from progressing under our own steam. God's "remembrance" of us from eternity reminds us that we were first conceived in His mind before we were ever born on earth, or the earth ever was. It was ordained that we would need God's grace and then His "mercy." Without grace, we would be unable to respond to God's call for rebelliousness is in our blood. Our hearts would be graciously softened before He would then pour out His mercy on us, not giving us what we deserved. Christ got what we deserved; He was punished for guilty old us. Away from prison Barabbas sped while Jesus for Barabbas bled.

The best man John could but point to Him, confess Him to be everything, acknowledge himself to be nothing. We too must confess that, without Jesus who is our life, we would be dead men walking, a mere heartbeat from hell.

ALL WHO LOOK

Our hearts are so encouraged because God both "spake" this world into existence and then "spake" His word into existence, through the lives and pens of living "fathers" of flesh and blood such as Abraham. None of "our fathers," even Abraham, in and of themselves were good enough to stand in God's presence due our first parents in the flesh. God would have been entirely righteous and justified to have cast us all into hell; but He did not—He would not abandon us.

Abraham was spoken to by God in a way which speaks to every called-out believer in "his" prophesied "seed" who would respond to God's word throughout place and time. Mary would be the one to bear this "seed" in her womb; John the Baptist would be the one to proclaim the coming of this "seed." Mary was the chosen and unique vessel, John the chosen forerunner and greatest prophet.

Man has his nuclear weaponry and biological warfare, his nanotechnology and satellite capabilities. God has placed such powers of genius in our hands; yet He does not need human instrumentality but chose through divine intervention to conceive a man within a woman's womb. God has ordained "his seed" to show us the exemplary life of righteousness. His chosen "seed" would bear the righteous wrath of God so that the sins of souls chosen in eternity would be saved without works; by grace through faith. If we are in this "seed" we have a citizenship in heaven and will be in a place to which can never earn admittance through our own human efforts, "for ever."

THE GOD-MAN

CHRIST RETURNED

"And Mary abode with her about three months, and returned to her own house." (Luke 1:56)

"Mary abode with her about three months." Christ Jesus would abide with us about three decades. He would minister to us, do miracles and speak parables in our midst for some three years. He would be permitted to dwell near John the Baptist whilst both were in the womb for "about three months." The enormity of this condescension cannot be put into words; we will surely be singing and talking about it in the glory to come; we'll never get tired of or bored of meditating on it.

Christ "returned" to heaven, a place in which He had, before creation, ever been. He "returned" to his "own house" for "Foxes have holes, and birds of the air *have* nests; but the Son of man hath not where to lay *his* head" (Luke 9:58) on this sin-drenched earth. The thing which so many of us, believers included, spend so much time thinking about and working for, Christ was content to lack.

We are frankly told about John's credentials: "Among them that are born of women there hath not risen a greater than John the Baptist: notwithstanding he that is least in the kingdom of heaven is greater than he" (Matt 11:11). Jesus would not dwell for long even with the best man ever born up to that time, but would return victorious to a kingdom better than any on earth.

In terms of typology, Mary the bearer of the "seed" from heaven, could not abide any longer with Elisabeth the bearer of the seed from earth. The God-man must go away, complete His work of salvific conquest so that the best man, unprofitable at best, may be renewed and go to dwell with Him in His "house."

At the time of writing, He has "returned" to His "own house" and is preparing a place for us which is better than any mind can conceive, "For since the beginning of the world *men* have not heard, nor perceived by the ear, neither hath the eye seen, O God, beside thee, *what* he hath prepared for him that waiteth for him." (Isa 64:4)

od-product-compliance